The Principles of Discipleship

The Principles of Discipleship

Paul Brewster

SUNESIS MINISTRIES LTD

The Principles of Discipleship

Copyright © 2017 Paul Brewster. The right of Paul Brewster to be identified as author of this work has been asserted by him in accordance with the Copyright, Designs, and Patents Act 1988. All rights reserved. No part of this publication may be reproduced or transmitted in any form or by any means, electronic or mechanical, including photocopy, recording, or any information storage and retrieval system, without permission in writing from the author.

ISBN 978-0-9956837-2-3

Published by Sunesis Ministries Ltd. For more information about Sunesis Ministries Ltd, please visit:

www.stuartpattico.com

Unless otherwise indicated, Bible quotations are from the Holy Bible, King James Version. Scripture quotations marked "Amp" are taken from the Amplified Bible, Copyright © 1954, 1958, 1962, 1964, 1965, 1987 by The Lockman Foundation. Used by permission. (www.Lockman.org). Scripture quotations marked "NKJV" are from the Holy Bible, New King James Version Copyright © 1982 Thomas Nelson, Inc. Used by permission. All rights reserved.

The author of this book does not dispense medical advice or prescribe the use of any technique as a form of treatment for physical, emotional, or medical problems without the advice of a physician, either directly or indirectly. The intent of the author is only to offer information of a general nature to help you in your quest for emotional and spiritual well-being. In the event you use any of the information in this book for yourself, the author and publisher assume no responsibility for your actions.

The views expressed in this book are solely those of the author and do not necessarily reflect the views of the publisher, and the publisher hereby disclaims any responsibility for them..

Contents

Introduction	8
Discipleship	10
Our Identity in Christ	16
The Trichotomy of the New Creation	22
The Necessity of the Atonement	31
Water Baptism	40
The Baptism with the Holy Spirit	48
Speaking in Tongues	58
Lord, Teach Us to Pray	67
How to Study the Bible	78
Meditating the Word	89
Spiritual Warfare	97
The Assembly of the Saints	110
Bibliography	119

I dedicate this book to my dear wife and best friend, Lorraine Brewster of 12 years. Our marriage is been enriched every year.

Introduction

Our Lord Jesus Christ, when on earth, uttered the following words which have echoed throughout the centuries and are the foundational principle of discipleship: "...If ye continue in my word, then are ye my disciples indeed; And ye shall know the truth, and the truth shall make you free" (Jn. 8:31-32). The key to true discipleship is to abide, to remain, to continue and to live in His Word, the catalyst to successfully following Jesus, the perfect example and model for every Christian. Then the next verse (v32) goes on to declare that you shall know the Truth and the Truth shall make you free.

Feeding on God's Word is at the very heart of discipleship, given the fact that the word "disciple" in the Greek rendering literally means "a learner". Its synonyms are student, pupil or scholar which conveys the meaning of discipleship: to learn and follow the instructions and teachings of our Lord as recorded in His Word. This principle is the foundation upon which all the other principles of discipleship are built. Without the Word of Truth, it is impossible to live life as a disciple of Jesus Christ.

The purpose of this book is to teach you the principles of discipleship that will conform your mind and heart into the image of Christ, which is the destiny of every believer (Rom. 8:29). Notice! I have cautiously used the word "principles" because principles relate to the thoughts, motives, intents and inner meaning rather than the outward and overt matters of Law, the purpose of which is to manipulate and control the outward behaviour of a person without transformation of the heart (Rom. 7; 8:3; Gal. 3:10, 19; 1 Tim. 1:9-10).

However, the discipleship principles are of grace and deals with the matters of the heart, transforming a person from the inside out through Christ's sacrificial work on the cross and the power of the Word of grace (Ac. 20:32; Eph. 2:8-10). At the very core of the successful Christian life is understanding your identity in Christ and recognising the sufficiency of the finished work of Calvary (2 Cor. 5:17; Eph. 2:10; Jn. 19:30; Col. 2:14-15).

As you read this book, I pray that the Holy Spirit will give understanding and wisdom of the principles in this book so that you are catapulted into the supernatural life and works prepared for you before the foundation of the world, and so walk in them (Eph. 2:10).

1

Discipleship

"Go ye therefore, and teach all nations, baptizing them in the name of the Father, and of the Son, and of the Holy Ghost: teaching them to observe all things whatsoever I have commanded you..." (Matt. 28:19-20a).

I think it is important to begin this topic of discipleship with the Great Commission which forms the basis upon which discipleship was taught and practised in the Early Church. It is discipleship that will fulfil the Great Commission in these last days. The opening verses unveil two aspects of discipleship: 1) the making of disciples (v19) and 2) the teaching of the principles of discipleship (v20).

THE MAKING OF DISCIPLES

In verse 19 the word "teach" is translated from the Greek rendering "matheteusate" which literally means to make disciples and is concomitant with the ordinance of baptism, alluding to the fact that water baptism is for disciples because Jesus says to make disciples and then baptise them.

In Mark's gospel account and version of the Great Commission, it says, "He that believeth and is baptized shall be saved..." (Mk. 16:16). As making disciples is used in association with baptism in Matthew's gospel account, believing is also used in connection with baptism that produces salvation. Baptism is one of the corresponding actions of genuine faith that produces salvation; water baptism does not save by itself but is an outward expression of an internal work of Grace. Notice! The verse does not say, "he that is baptised shall be saved" but baptism is preceded by believing.

The Gospel of Mark shows us that believing the gospel that is preached saves a sinner from damnation, makes him a disciple of Jesus Christ and qualifies him for water baptism which is the answer of a good conscience towards God (1 Pe. 3:21). It confirms a believer's good conscience in the sight of God, and it's in this sense that baptism saves a person.

Matthew and Mark's account make it clear that a person becomes a disciple of Jesus Christ when they repent and believe the gospel of Jesus Christ. To become a disciple is tantamount to becoming a Christian from a true biblical perspective. According to Acts 11:26, the disciples at Antioch were first called Christians. Therefore a Christian is a disciple and a disciple is a Christian. So once people become disciples or Christians, the next responsibility of the Great Commission is to teach them the truths and principles of discipleship mentioned in the Word of God.

TEACHING THE PRINCIPLES AND TRUTHS OF DISCIPLESHIP

Now, once people have become disciples, which in the Greek is "mathetes", meaning learners, students and pupils, then it is the responsibility of the leadership and the church to teach them the Word of God as commanded by our Lord:

"Teaching them to observe all things whatsoever I have commanded you..." (Matt. 28:20).

New converts need to be taught how to live out the principles of discipleship taught by Jesus Christ, and not be left to fend for themselves, or else they will eventually die spiritually and return to the world from which they were once saved. On the other hand, the responsibility of new converts is to desire the sincere milk of the Word that they may grow spiritually (1 Pe. 2:2).

New converts who begin their Christian life and status as students need to be taught and equipped with revelation knowledge of God's Word so that they can grow and mature in Christ Jesus (Eph. 4:11-13). Sinners, who enter God's Kingdom through the new birth (Jn. 3:3-5) must understand that they are students called to learn how the Kingdom works and begin to function according to its laws and principles by renewing the mind (Rom. 12:2).

People who enrol to do specific courses become students and their responsibility is to learn about the topic on which they have enrolled. They will have to attend classes, listen to their teachers' lectures, read articles, books and other relevant materials, and get experience of vocation on placements. Yet, there are some students who would not take advantage of acquiring the knowledge available through study and diligence, even though they hold the status of student. There is a difference between student status and truly functioning as a student through diligent study and learning.

In the same vein, you have Christians who are disciples in status, but do not truly grow or develop through diligent study of the Word of God. However, those who learn and apply the Word to their lives are truly functioning as disciples, learners and students of the Word. Jesus instructs us to take His yoke upon us and learn of Him so that we may find rest for our souls (Matt. 11:29).

A yoke is an instrument for labour upon which two animals of the same kind are joined together. By salvation through Christ, We are joined to His yoke; that is, Jesus bears the yoke with us because we are joined unto Him as one spirit – partaker of His divine nature, His image and likeness (1 Cor. 6:17; 2 Pe. 1:4; 1 Jn. 4:17). Therefore being of His kind and yoked together with Christ, it is easy to learn of Him since it is in our nature to do the Word. The teaching and principles of the Word are not for the unconverted because you cannot put new wine in old wineskins. You cannot teach spiritual principles to the unregenerate; he must be born again. That is why the Great Commission tells us to make disciples and then teach them all things (Matt. 28:19-20).

Jesus spoke to the Jews that believed in Him saying,

"...If ye continue in my word, then are ye my disciples indeed; And ye shall know the truth, and the truth shall make you free"

(Jn. 8:31b-32).

To comprehend the meaning and application of these verses, you must first understand the context - the situation and the Jewish audience to whom He is speaking. The context tells us that there were Jews who believed on Him (v31a), but did not act on His Word to become His true disciples, for in verse 33, their response to Jesus' statement was not positive, neither did they understand what He was saying.

Many Jews believed on Jesus because of the miracle of Lazarus being raised from death. As a result, they welcomed Him into Jerusalem as the King of Israel, casting down branches of palm trees before Him; and yet, later on, cried out for Him to be crucified. Why? They abode not in His Word that they might be saved.

Also among the chief rulers, many believed on Him, but because of the Pharisees, they did not act on His Word by confessing him, for fear of being excommunicated from the synagogues; the reason being, they loved the praise of men more than the praise of God (Jn. 12:42-43). To be a disciple, there must be a denial of self and take up your cross to follow Jesus (Matt. 16:24-26).

The Jews who believed, as seen in the two previous examples, did not act upon the Word of God for them to abide in it and for it to abide in them. Being born again of the Word (1 Pe. 1:23) deposits that Word to abide in you, and you to abide in it in order to become a true disciple as Jesus said,

"...If ye continue [Gk meno: abide] in my words, then are ye my disciples indeed; and ye shall know the truth, and the truth shall make you free" (Jn. 8:31-32).

The context of freedom is freedom from the slavery of sin (v34). Whoever is in Christ is a true disciple and has been made free from sin and now needs to grow and develop in the knowledge of the Word to understand who he is in Christ and what he can do through Him who gives him strength (Philip. 4:13).

2

Our Identity in Christ

Therefore if any man be in Christ, he is a new creature: old things are passed away; behold, all things are become new" (2 Cor. 5:17).

It is true that how a person lives out their life will be determined by how they perceive themselves: who am I? Where did I come from? What is my purpose for being here? What inherent abilities and skills do I have? And what course of direction should I take in life? These are some of the questions that many people ask themselves. Those answer elude them. But thanks be to God that these answers can be found in Him for He is the Architect and Creator of every one of us, and in Christ Who is the Wisdom of God, we can tap into His wisdom to find out these answers which are all tied up in understanding our identity in Christ (2 Cor. 5:17).

There are certain core truths that are key to understanding your personal identity in Christ: - knowing who you are in Him; what you can do through Him, and what you possess in Him. These are the three foundational truths upon which you can build a strong, vibrant and successful Christian life. The structure of a building is only as strong as its foundation. A strong foundation will mean a strong building.

Desire and absorb voraciously, the biblical understanding of your Christian identity based on these three foundational truths that will be covered in this book.

THE NEW CREATION IN CHRIST.

In the opening verse of Scripture, the Apostle shares by the Spirit concerning who we are "in Christ" whose Greek rendering is "en Christo", a phrase used exclusively by the Apostle Paul. It was unique in his understanding of the mystery of Christ that was hidden before the foundation of the world (Eph. 3:4-6). For in Christ, we are made partakers of His unsearchable riches by the Gospel (v9).
There are numerous passages in the Pauline epistles that teach about believers being in Christ – just to list a few: Romans 8:1-2, 39; 1 Corinthians 15:22; Ephesians 2:10; 1 Thessalonians 4:16). The phrase "en Christo", encapsulates specific benefits to being in Christ, of which the opening verse of this chapter intimates:

"If any man be in Christ, he is a new [creation]: old things are passed away; behold, all things are become new" (2 Cor. 5:17).

This verse shows us who we really are in Christ. When you committed your heart and life to Jesus by believing with your heart and confessing with your mouth that Jesus Christ died for your sins and rose again for your justification, you were translated from being in Adam to now being in Christ (1 Cor. 15:22). You are now a new creation in Christ Jesus; the old things of your former life - the old you and your old sins, are passed away by the cleansing blood of Jesus, and you have become a new person created anew by the work of the Holy Spirit (Titus 3:5).

It is a work that took place on the inside; within the core or essence of your being called the heart or the human spirit - a promise that was spoken of concerning Israel's national and spiritual redemption:

"Then will I sprinkle clean water upon you, and ye shall be clean: from all your filthiness, and from all your idols, will I cleanse you. A new heart also will I give you, and a new spirit will I put within you: and I will take away the stony heart out of your flesh, and I will give you an heart of flesh" (Ezek. 36:25-26).

In the work of redemption, we become partakers of the blessings promised to Israel (Eph. 2:12-19). We have been cleansed on the inside from every filthiness of sin, by the water of the Word (Eph. 5:26; Jn. 15:3). Before the new birth, our spirits were dead to God separated from a vital relationship with Him: the Source of life. But when we received by faith, the Gospel, the sinful nature was put to death and removed from our spirit, and we received a new nature – a new heart and a new spirit – becoming alive unto God (Eph. 2:1).

By being born of the Spirit (Jn. 3:3-8), we became a new creation in Christ Jesus; no longer sinners separated from God but children of the Most High, created in righteousness and true holiness (Eph. 2:22-24). So when the Apostle Paul addressed the believers in Christ, He said they are a new creation, old things have passed away, behold, all things have become new. This is the precise tense in the Greek language.

Therefore, when you read 2 Corinthians 5:17, it is stating who you really are in Christ irrespective of how guilty or condemned you may feel about your past. You are now a new creation. God is no longer holding anything against you for He remembers your sins no more (Jer. 31:34).

You are God's unique masterpiece created in Christ Jesus unto good works. The world says, "Who you are begins with what you do"; but the antithesis of that, is what the Scripture supports: what you do begins with who you are. Ephesians 2:10 states,

"For we are his workmanship created in Christ Jesus unto good works, which God hath before ordained that we should walk in them."

Since God is perfect in wisdom and power, anything that he does is perfect and complete (Deut. 32:4), therefore if you are God's workmanship, you are His perfect masterpiece created in Christ Jesus, the sinless, Holy One. In your recreated, rejuvenated human spirit, you are perfect and complete in Christ (Col. 2:10). God sees you in Christ as perfect and righteous as Jesus is (1 Jn. 4:17); a unique and priceless work. The psalmist declares,

"I will praise thee, for I am fearfully and wonderfully made: marvellous are thy works; and that my soul knoweth right well" (Ps. 139:14).

David reflects on God's awesome, creative power and wisdom,

and makes a statement about himself concerning this fact, how he is fearfully and wonderfully made: thus speaking of his physical make-up and power of cognitive reasoning. It also has a spiritual application within the realm of the spirit. As a new creation in Christ Jesus, You are God's awesome and wonderful masterpiece; a composite of abilities, gifts, talents and skills unique to every individual who is called by God to fulfil the purpose of why they were born in the earth (Rom. 8:28).

Ephesians 2:10 affirms that we have been created unto good works in accordance with His preordained purpose. That purpose is threefold: 1) It is redemptive, 2) it is for the common good of all, and 3) its ultimate purpose is for the glory of God.
In creation, God has built in every living thing a genetic code to function, distinct from other species. For example, He has deposited a genetic code for one kind of species to fly and another to live and swim under waters. One is natural to birds, the other is natural to fish. Both functions are natural to them. A bird does not try to fly neither does a fish try to swim. They just do it because it is been put in their genetic code by their Creator.

In the same vein, God deposited in your spirit a divine genetic code when you were born again to perform supernatural acts for the Kingdom of God, that transcends natural ability. Because of becoming a new creation, endowed with supernatural abilities, gifts and talents, you are able to function beyond natural reasoning where the supernatural becomes natural to you. Therefore, whatever the Word of God says you can do, you can do it, even when it does not make sense You are called by God to do the impossible and to live an extraordinary life (Mk. 9:23).

Being in Christ is a testimony to the fact that we are just like

Him; we can do what He did; as joint-heirs with Christ, we possess what He possessed. By the new birth and the promise of the Holy Spirit, we are equipped to follow everything that our Lord taught us in His Word to be and to do (Matt. 28:20). It is already in you to do the Word, unlike the world which is dead in trespasses and sins (Eph. 2:1-5). That is why it is futile to teach discipleship principles to an unregenerate world, for that would be like putting a cart before a horse.

Discipleship training for believers is trichotomous: teaching who they are in Christ, what they possess in Him, and what they can do through Him. The Law showed us what we could not do (Rom. 7) so we would put our trust in another – that is Christ Jesus (Gal. 4:24). Develop a new creation conscious mentality through the Word so that you may function accordingly. What you focus on and give your attention to will produce corresponding actions.

There are foundational truths you need to know about being a new creation in Christ. Knowing these will give you a firm footing upon which to build a strong and successful Christian life.

3

The Trichotomy of the New Creation

"And such were some of you: but ye are washed, but ye are sanctified, but ye are justified in the name of the Lord Jesus, and by the Spirit of our God" (1 Cor. 6:11).

In the opening verse of scripture, there are three related aspects to the new creation in Christ Jesus that the Apostle Paul lists as follows: "...ye are washed...ye are sanctified...ye are justified in the name of the Lord Jesus, and by the Spirit of our God" (ibid.). Understanding these foundational truths are key to knowing who you are in Christ and building a strong, vibrant and successful Christian life.

The context of the previous verses (v9, 10) indicates the kinds of people who will not inherit the Kingdom of God such as the sexually immoral, idol worshippers, homosexuals, thieves, covetous, drunkards etc., of which Paul said were some of you, lost and without God. But the Apostle proceeded further to say to the believers of Corinth that they are washed, sanctified and justified in the name of Jesus and the Spirit of God. That was the transition from the kingdom of darkness into the Kingdom of light; from not inheriting to inheriting the Kingdom of God (Col. 1:12-13).

The transition from the old to the new, from death to life and from darkness to Light occurred by washing, sanctification and justification through the name of Jesus Christ and the Spirit of our God. Therefore, I want to show you from the Scripture the importance and significance of each and how they relate to our new identity in Christ.

YOU ARE WASHED

In Titus 3:3-6, it explains what this washing is and how we were cleansed from all our sins:

"for we ourselves also were sometimes foolish, disobedient, deceived, serving divers lusts and pleasures, living in malice and envy, hateful, and hating one another. But after that the kindness and love of God our Saviour toward man appeared, Not by works of righteousness which we have done, but according to his mercy he saved us, by the washing of regeneration and renewing of the Holy Ghost; which he shed on us abundantly through Jesus Christ our Saviour;"

The washing identified in 1 Corinthians 6:11 is explained in the above passage of scripture to be the washing of regeneration and renewing of the Holy Ghost. That is the experience that transitions a person from the old sinful nature – the root of old things – into newness of life, by a new heart and a new spirit (Ezek.

36:26) Old things passing away included the old sinful nature, called the old man, and the old sins (Rom. 6:3-6; Eph. 4:22-24; 2 Pe. 1:9).

Regeneration is from the Greek rendering "palingenesia", which is derived from two Greek words: "palin", meaning "again", and "genesis", meaning "birth", hence, regeneration refers to a rebirth, a new birth – being born again. In the first birth, we were born of the flesh which can be seen by the optical eye. However, being born again of the Spirit is spiritual and unseen by the physical sense (Jn. 3:8).

In the natural birth, we were born with a sinful nature, but in the new birth, we were born with a new nature that is holy and righteous (Eph. 4:24). By being born of the flesh, we were born descended of Adam, but in the new birth, we are born descendants of Christ (1 Cor. 15:22) As we were partakers with Adam in the consequences of his sin, we are now joint-heirs with Christ in the blessings of His obedience (Gen. 3; Rom. 5:12-21).

Regeneration is an instantaneous work and divine act of the Holy Spirit based upon the shed blood of Jesus Christ, whereby our old sinful nature is washed away and replaced with a new heart and a new spirit that is alive unto God (Ezek. 36:26). There is no more sinful nature in you and no more guilt to account for since old things are passed away. There is therefore no condemnation to those who are in Christ (Rom. 8:1) because in Christ, you are a new creation having been made alive and renewed by the Holy Spirit (2 Cor. 5:17; Titus 3:5). No believer retains an old sinful nature after conversion, for old things have passed away.

The internal evidences of regeneration are: 1) belief that Jesus is the Christ, the Son of God (1 Jn. 5:1, 4-5); 2) love for Christ and your fellow brethren (Jn. 8:42; 1 Jn. 3:14); 3) the Holy Spirit bears witness with your spirit that you are a child of God (Rom. 8:16).

External evidences are: 1) works of righteousness (1 Jn. 2:29); 2) the Christian will not live in sin and in the old habits of the old life (1 Jn. 3:5-6); 3) the born again believer will overcome the world (1 Jn. 5:4); the Christian believer knows God (1 Jn. 4:7).

YOU ARE SANCTIFIED

"But we are bound to give thanks always to God for you, brethren beloved of the Lord, because God hath from the beginning chosen you to salvation through sanctification of the Spirit and belief of the truth:" (2 Thess. 2:13).

Another aspect of our identity is that we have been sanctified in Christ Jesus. All those who are saved are sanctified because the above verse affirms that we have been chosen to salvation through sanctification of the Spirit and belief of the truth; hence, you have the divine responsibility performed by the Spirit, and you have also the human responsibility to believe the truth. At the point of believing the truth, you were sanctified by the Spirit.

According to the context of the scriptural passage, the truth that you believed was the gospel, as stated in verse 14,

"Whereunto he called you by our gospel, to the obtaining of the glory of our Lord Jesus Christ".

Also read verses 11-12 of the same passage which states that those who are damned receive not the love of the truth that they might be saved. Therefore according to the passage, you cannot be saved and not sanctified, and vice versa. The fact that you are saved means that you are sanctified.

The basic meaning of the term "sanctify" in the Hebrew and Greek languages of the Bible is "to set apart or to consecrate unto". In Scripture, the term sanctification was used in reference to persons, animals, places, objects, days, and seasons.

Levites were set apart and consecrated unto God for Temple worship and service. Jesus Christ set apart or consecrated Himself unto God for the work of redemption – His imminent sufferings and death on the cross for the salvation of mankind (Jn. 17:19).

In heathen worship, the Hebrew term "to sanctify", referred to sodomites and temple prostitutes who were set apart unto the service of false gods and immoral practices. Nevertheless, in the Judeo-Christian faith, sanctification conveyed the moral and ethical meaning of holiness and purity in reference to Christian believers. The reason it carried this idea is because that which is set apart unto God who is holy, pure and perfect, becomes a partaker of the nature and character of the One unto whom he is consecrated.

Therefore, sanctification conveys the ethical idea of holiness, spiritual cleansing and moral purity. That is why Christian believers are called saints (Gk hagioi) whose Greek adjective is akin to the Greek verb "sanctify" (Gk hagiazo). And so those who have been sanctified by the blood of Jesus Christ have been set apart from the defilement of sin through spiritual cleansing and consecrated unto God and His holiness of character. 1 Peter 1:15-16 states,

"but as he which hath called you is holy, so be ye holy in all manner of conversation; Because it is written, Be ye holy for I am holy."

Sanctification, as described in several Scriptural passages, is a state which the believer has already attained, because of being created in true holiness (Eph. 4:24) through conversion (Ac. 20:32; 26:18; Rom. 15:16; 1 Cor. 1:2; 6:11; Jude 1:1). There is no progressive or future sanctification for believers. It is a state already attained and holiness is what believers are called to be and walk in. Because we are sanctified, we are suppose to grow spiritually unto perfection (1 Pe. 2:2; Eph. 4:13-14; Matt. 5:48).

The Apostle Paul referred to the Corinthian believers as sanctified (1 Cor. 1:2) and at the same time rebuked them for their carnality and imperfections (1 Cor. 3:1-3). The Corinthian believers' carnality was not an issue of having a sinful nature, for they were already created in righteousness and true holiness (Eph. 4:22-24; Col. 3:9-10). Rather, the issue was of an unrenewed mind that needed to be trained in the Word of God to conform its behaviour to the holy nature on the inside, where the outward behaviour and thought life would be consistent with their new nature within.

A believer's carnality is a result of immaturity and the need to grow spiritually and live out the new life he received in Christ Jesus when he was born again (1 Cor. 3:1-2; Heb. 5:12-14; 1 Pe. 2:2). It is about growing in the consciousness and knowledge of everything that resides within him in Christ Jesus that will become activated in his life (Philm. 1:6). How you understand your identity in Christ will determine how you live out the new life within. Nevertheless, there will be a continual fight going on within the believer – not a struggle between two natures, but a struggle between two opposing principles of flesh and Spirit (Gal. 5:16-23).

YE ARE JUSTIFIED

"Therefore being justified by faith, we have peace with God through our Lord Jesus Christ" (Rom. 5:1).

The third important aspect of the new creation in Christ Jesus is that we have been justified by faith in our Lord Jesus Christ. That includes the Person of Jesus Christ and His finished work on the cross of Calvary. Justification is what the atoning death of Jesus Christ made provision for since humanity was unable to be justified on its own merits by virtue of the fact that we were sinners who needed a Saviour (Rom. 5:8; 3:23). Justification is one of the central doctrines of both the Old and New Testaments which shows us how a righteous and holy God can justify sinners who have violated His holy Law. Before examining this, it is important to have a correct understanding of the term "justify".

The Greek word for "justify" is "dikaioo", which means to exhibit, to evince, to show, to declare or pronounce one to be right or righteous. It is the expression of counting, deeming, or regarding someone to be righteous. This word is applied to God or man. However, its meaning is never used to make a person righteous. You may ask the question: "How does a righteous God justify a sinner?" To begin to answer the question, it is important to note that the doctrine of justification is inseparably related to the sacrificial and substitutionary death of Jesus Christ.

In the opening verse of this chapter, it reads, "Therefore being [declared righteous] by faith, we have peace with God through our Lord Jesus Christ" (Rom. 5:1). This verse reveals the moral basis for justifying a sinner and the means by which it is applied.

THE MORAL BASIS FOR JUSTIFICATION

The moral basis for justification is found in the Person and work of Jesus Christ. His Person was both divine and human, therefore His divine and human nature were vital to the accomplishment of the work of redemption. In His divine nature, he was the Son of God (Jn. 1:1-3, 14; 10:30; 1 Tim. 3:16). God who gave man spiritual life is the only One who could restore it back to him. Therefore, God came as Jesus Christ, to restore that which was lost. Only the Divine is the Source of life and so the restoration of life could only come from Him (Jn. 1:1-3, 14; 3:16; 1 Jn. 5:11-12).

Because God took on human form (Philip. 2:5-7), it was therefore possible for Him to take upon Himself the legal guilt and punishment for sin, which is death, so that all sinners who believe in Him would not perish but have eternal life. Jesus took our penalty upon Himself so that we may be free. This is the work He came to accomplish. Through His sacrificial death on the cross, the divine charges against us have been acquitted; we are not guilty. God has declared us righteous because he looks on us as if we had fulfilled the Law and had never sinned.

You may ask, "how can a holy God look upon us as if we had

never sinned?" Well, by faith in the finished work of Christ's sacrificial death, God has charged the righteousness of Jesus Christ - the One who never sinned – to our account as a free gift (Rom. 5:17). Every believer is the righteousness of God in Christ Jesus. Irrespective of your past and your shortcomings, you are perfectly righteous in Christ from the day you received Him as your personal saviour (2 Cor. 5:21). This is what Justification did for everyone who was born again.

The means by which justification is applied is by faith alone. The Hebrew writer affirms that without faith, it is impossible to please God, for this is how the elders obtained a good testimony that they were righteous (Heb. 11:1-6). Abraham's faith was counted unto him for righteousness, who is the father of us all (Rom. 4). Putting your faith in the Person and work of Jesus Christ will be regarded unto you for righteousness because the moral basis for our justification is twofold:

1) the Person of Jesus Christ which has two aspects: a) believing He was Divine – the Son of the living God – b) believing that He came in the flesh (Jn. 1:1-3, 14; 3:16-18, 36; 10:30).
2) the work of Christ in redemption is threefold: a) He died for our sins (Rom. 4:25a); b) He rose again for our justification (Rom. 4:25b; and c) he is seated at the right hand of God making intercession for us (Rom. 8:34).

4

The Necessity of the Atonement

"Surely he hath borne our griefs, and carried our sorrows: yet we did esteem him stricken, smitten of God, and afflicted. But he was wounded for our transgressions, he was bruised for our iniquities: the chastisement of our peace was upon him; and with his stripes we are healed. All we like sheep have gone astray; we have turned every one to his own way; and the LORD hath laid on him the iniquity of us all" (Is. 53:4-6).

In human life and experience, it is true that where there is a solution, it is because there was a problem. So it is in the realm of the spirit. A serious problem emerged in God's created universe that required a divine solution to save mankind from ultimate ruin and destruction. That problem was sin, and the solution to that problem was Jesus Christ.

In the beginning of time, God created the world and gave His unique creation: man to have dominion over all living creatures, plant life and resources that were upon the earth (Gen. 1:26-30). There was total harmony and peace upon the earth; a world free from sufferings, pain and death. In God's eyes, everything was good (v31). Man had an intimate relationship with God as long as he remained obedient to Him. There was no lack. Every herb and tree bearing fruit was given to him for food except for one – the tree of the knowledge of good and evil. A divine injunction was given:

"And the LORD God commanded the man saying, Of every tree of the garden thou mayest freely eat: But of the tree of the knowledge of good and evil, thou shalt not eat of it: for in the day that thou eatest thereof thou shalt surely die" (Gen. 2:16-17).

The divine command carried with it the penalty of death, if disobeyed. Transgressing God's command would set in motion a law called the law of sin and death.

This law is mentioned numerous times in both the Old and New Testaments (Deut. 27:15-26; 30:15; Rom. 6:23; 8:2) you will also see its effect throughout biblical history: from Genesis to Revelation. It is a law that has plagued humanity for centuries up until this present day: violence, wars, strife, rebellion, murders, thefts, adulteries, sexual immorality, lying, sickness and diseases, famine, poverty etc. these are the consequences of sin entering our world by our human ancestors (Gen. 3; Rom. 5:12-19).

The universal law of God is echoed throughout the ages: "... the soul that sinneth, it shall die...For the wages of sin is death..." (Ezek. 18:4d; Rom. 6:23a). There are three dimensions to death 1) spiritual death – where a person is dead and separated in his spirit from the life and fellowship of God (Eph. 2:1-5); 2) physical death which is separation of the spirit from the body (Gen. 3:19; Ja. 2:26a); and 3) the second death is eternal separation from the Presence of God to the tormenting Lake of fire (Rev. 19:20; 20:11-15).

The Law, even the Ten Commandments, was given by God to show us explicitly that we could not keep them perfectly (Ex. 20) and to teach us that we could not find salvation in ourselves but in another (Rom. 5:20; 7). The ultimate penalty for any sin is always death because you are dealing with a perfect, holy and righteous God who will judge your life according to His perfect standard of righteousness. Since God is holy and just, sin will have to be punished either sooner or later.

The Law with its legal requirements and punitive justice taught Israel that any sin – sins of ignorance - committed against the Law required the killing of an innocent sacrificial victim to atone for the sin and the sinner What was used to graphically depict this was blood (Lev. 17:11). Paul the Apostle, states in the Book of Hebrews,

"And almost all things are by the law purged with blood; and without the shedding of blood is no remission" (Heb. 9:22).

In Levitical and sacrificial terms, blood being shed represents an innocent life given up in death on behalf of a sinner, releasing him from the legal penalty. Here, we are taught about God's love and righteous justice. God's righteous justice demands death, but His love makes provision for it. The Lord will not violate His own justice to be merciful, anymore than He would compromise His holiness to consent with sin for man's sake.

Every member of humanity throughout history begotten of man has sinned and come under the guilt of God's righteous standard (Rom. 3:9-20, 23). The Apostle Paul on his theology in the Epistle to the Romans conclude that both Jews and Gentiles are guilty before God so that He might be merciful to both (Rom. 1-3). And so now we come to the necessity of the atoning death of Christ; He died for us bearing the legal guilt and punishment for our sins so that we may be freed from them (Rom. 5:8). Moreover, as the legal penalty was death, Jesus tasted death for every man to redeem us from it (Heb. 2:9). By analogy, if you were fined for violating a traffic law, the Law would require you to pay that fine in spite of your inability to pay it. However, someone comes along and pays the fine for you, consequently freeing you from the debt. That is what Jesus did when He died for us, taking that burden upon Himself and liberating us from it.

There are three essential truths about the necessity of the sacrificial death of Christ: 1) God is holy and righteous, therefore His wrath against sin needs to be appeased; 2) humanity is essentially depraved because of sin; and 3) the only way of approaching God is through the blood (death) of a pure, innocent, spotless victim – Jesus Christ. These truths are shadowed in the Old Testament sacrificial system (Jn. 1:17; Col. 2:16-17; Heb. 10:1). Jesus come on the scene of human history declaring,

"...I am the way, the truth, and the life: no man cometh unto the Father, but by me" (Jn. 14:6).

Jesus Christ is the only true and acceptable sacrifice by which one may approach God and obtain life. He is the true way to eternal life.

THE SUFFICIENCY OF THE CROSS

"Blessed be the God and Father of our Lord Jesus Christ, who hath blessed us with all spiritual blessings in heavenly places in Christ" (Eph. 1:3).

Everything you will ever need or require to live a successful Christian life and fulfil your divine assignment has already been provided for in Christ Jesus. There is no challenge in life that you will face that God has not already given you the spiritual resources to overcome. These resources are called spiritual blessings. God the Father is the Source of all spiritual blessings, and Jesus Christ is the means by which these blessings are made available to us. The terms "blessed" and "blessings" literally mean "to speak well of," or in other words to say a good word. In this lies the revelation of how blessings are released. God has released blessings through His Word and Jesus Christ has confirmed and ratified it in His own blood. Any benefit said to be in Christ has been sanctioned in the Person of Jesus Christ and His redemptive work on the cross.

All spiritual blessings are made available to us by Jesus Christ and His finished work of redemption. Galatians 3:13-14 declares,

"Christ hath redeemed us from the curse of the law, being made a curse for us: for it is written, Cursed is every one that hangeth on a tree: That the blessing of Abraham might come on the Gentiles through Jesus Christ; that we might receive the promise of the Spirit through faith."

Christ redeemed us from the curse of the Law by becoming a curse in our stead so that the blessing of Abraham that was due

Him came upon us – the Gentiles. The curse of the Law is death, whose actual reference was for anyone who committed a sin worthy of death was put to death and hanged on a tree (Deut. 21:22-23). Similarly, Jesus was accursed of God for the sins of the world, bearing in His own body the penalty of death so that we would experience the Abrahamic blessings as descendants of Abraham (Gen. 12:3).

The concept of the blessing in Ephesians 1:3 is threefold: firstly, we are to bless – to speak well of – God with praises and thanksgiving for what he has already given us (1 Cor. 14:16-17); secondly, because He has spoken words of blessings upon us in His Word (2 Cor. 1:20); and thirdly, the Greek definition of the blessing is "to cause to prosper." We are partake of the benefits of those blessings for God's Word does not return to Him void of power. The spoken Word of God empowers us to prosper through the precious blood of Jesus Christ. The Word and the blood has already made provision for our blessings.

Jesus suffered and died for us; His death on the cross was sufficient. Nothing needs to be added to the work of the cross and nothing needs to be taken away. Jesus accomplished a perfect and complete work. His words uttered from the cross, "It is finished" (Jn. 19:30) has reverberated down through the centuries stating that our sins are paid in full for all time; no more condemnation (Rom. 8:1, sin has no more power over us. Every blessing is already provided for through Christ and his work on the cross.

Isaiah's prophecy in the 53rd chapter concerning the suffering Servant-Messiah shows us the sufficiency of His benefits as a product of His sufferings and death on our behalf,

"Surely, he hath borne our griefs, and carried our sorrows: yet we did esteem him stricken, smitten of God, and afflicted - But he was wounded for our transgressions, he was bruised for our iniquities: the chastisement of our peace was upon him; and with his stripes we are healed" (Is. 53:4-5).

Everything that God has promised us comes through the Blood of the Cross (Col. 1:20). In the bible passage above, Jesus bore our griefs and carried our sorrows. The words "borne" and "carried" in the Hebrew rendering convey the idea of one taking the burden of another, placing it upon himself and carrying it away so that the other may be free from it. This was the purpose of the atonement of Jesus Christ, to bear and carry away our burdens so that we do not have to bear them.

What did he carry to remove from us? He bore away our griefs and sorrows. In the Hebrew language, griefs is translated from "choliy", meaning sicknesses, diseases; and "sorrows" is from the Hebrew term "makob", which denotes pains. Therefore, the scriptural passage tells us that Jesus bore away our sicknesses, diseases and carried our pains, of which the result is concluded by: "...with his stripes we are healed" (v5). The sacrifice and sufferings of Jesus removed the very things that He took upon Himself (see Matt. 8:16-17; 1 Pe. 2:24).

Jesus also carried away our sins because the same Hebrew term used for bearing away our sicknesses is also used for Him taking away our sins (v6, 11, 12). He bore our sins in the wounds and bruises inflicted on His body. Verse 5 states,

"he was wounded for our transgressions, he was bruised for our iniquities..."

In the New Testament, it declares that Jesus bore our sins in His own body on the tree (1 Pe. 2:24a), consequently ushering us into a life of forgiveness and justification: - "...by his knowledge shall my righteous servant justify many; for he shall bear their iniquities" (v11).

The following clause of verse 5 also declares,

"...the chastisement of our peace was upon him..."

Jesus was chastised and punished for our peace. Peace in the Hebrew language is the word "shalom", and it is derived from the Hebrew root: shalem meaning to be complete, whole and sound. The general meaning behind shalem is that of completeness and fulfilment; a state of wholeness, unity and restored relationship, and notion of restoration of peace through payment (Josh. 10:1; Ex. 21:36). Its derivative "shalom", is comprehensive in its meaning and denotes peace, prosperity, wellbeing, health, completeness and safety. It is equally as wide in meaning as the Hebrew word for salvation.

The broad sense of shalom is the extent to which Jesus Christ made provision through His sufferings and death on the cross. Therefore, the provision peace made available to us through the atonement of Jesus includes:

- a restoration of relationship with God (Rom. 5:1)
- restoration of relationship with fellowmen (Eph. 2:13-16)
- peace and soundness of mind (Rom. 8:6; Philip. 4:5-9)
- holistic prosperity: - prospering spiritually, mentally,

- physically and financially (3 Jn. 2; Rom. 8:6; 2 Cor. 8:9; 9:8; Matt. 6:33)
- emotional wellbeing (Neh. 8:10; Philip. 4:4)
- health (1 Pe. 2:24; 3 Jn. 2)
- safety of spirit, soul and body (1 Thess. 5:23; Ps. 91; 121)
- a state of completeness where there is nothing missing and nothing broken (Col. 2:10; 2 Cor. 1:20).

The bible teaches that all the promises of God in Christ are yes and amen. Nothing needs to be added because nothing is missing for our sufficiency is of God through Christ and His work of redemption. Furthermore, if God did not spare His most precious possession – His own Son, but delivered Him up to death shall He not with Him freely give us all things (Rom 8:32)? Therefore, let us grow in the understanding of what Jesus accomplished for us by learning and feeding voraciously on the Word so that we may appropriate all that Christ has provided for us.

5

Water Baptism

"know ye not, that so many of us as were baptised into Jesus Christ were baptised into his death? Therefore we are buried with him by baptism into death: that like as Christ was raised up from the dead by the glory of the Father, even so we also should walk in newness of life. For if we have been planted together in the likeness of his death, we shall be also in the likeness of his resurrection" (Rom. 6:3-5).

Water baptism is an ordinance that was commanded by Jesus just prior to His ascension into heaven. It is part of the Great Commission enjoined to the church, therefore baptism is not optional. Jesus commanded the church saying,

" Go ye therefore, and teach [Gk make disciples] of all nations, baptizing them in the name of the Father, and of the Son, and of the Holy Ghost... Go into all the world, and preach the gospel to every creature. He that believeth and is baptized shall be saved; but he that believeth not shall be damned" (Matt. 28:19; Mk.

16:15-16).

In Matthew's Gospel, the disciples are commanded by Jesus to baptise, and in Mark's Gospel, the sinners response to the gospel is to believe and be baptised. So every sinner who comes to Christ should be baptised as part of their salvation experience. Now, every new convert should experience and understand the significance of baptism.

Baptism comes from the Greek word "baptisma", which consists of the threefold process of immersion, submersion and emergence. So water baptism entails the immersing and submersing in water followed by emerging out of the water, and the Greek term is derived from the word "bapto", meaning "to dip." By definition, the threefold process of baptism reveals the spiritual significance of Christian baptism. The immersion represents the believer's death with Christ; the submersion signifies the believer's burial with Christ; and the emergence denotes the believer's resurrection with Christ as stated in the opening verses of this chapter (Rom. 6:3-5). The Christian believer is identified with Christ in His death, burial and resurrection. Therefore, the only true method of baptism is immersion, not sprinkling, as it does not symbolically convey the idea of death, burial and resurrection.

The first introduction of water baptism was in the ministry of John the Baptist, whose baptism was a baptism unto repentance as he said,

""I indeed baptize you with water unto [into] repentance..." (Matt. 3:11).

John's message and baptism conveyed the need of his hearers to repent because the Kingdom of heaven was here. Repentance was the prerequisite to entering the Kingdom (Matt. 3:1-2). The Greek word for "repentance" is "metanoia", meaning to change your mind, resulting in turning away from one's sins unto God. John the Baptist stressed to his religious audience that repentance was necessary before coming to be baptised (v7-8). He said,

"Bring forth therefore fruits meet for repentance" (Matt. 3:8).

Another Bible version makes this verse clearer and brings out the Greek sense,

"Bring forth fruit that is consistent with repentance [let your lives prove your change of heart]" (Matt. 3:8 Amp).

And in the Williams New Testament, it declares,

"But when he saw many of the Pharisees and Sadducees coming for baptism, he said to them, "You brood of vipers, who warned you to escape from the wrath that is coming? Produce then, fruit that is consistent with the repentance you profess" (v7-8).

John refused to baptise those who came to his baptism until he saw fruit, that is, actions consistent with repentance. In the scriptural passage, he denied baptism to the Pharisees and Sadducees until they had proven their repentance by their deeds. You may ask, 'Why'? The answer is because water baptism is an ordinance: an external, outward rite that is symbolic of a true internal, inward work of Grace in the heart. The outward is supposed to be an expression of its spiritual counterpart. Only those who have truly repented and believed should be baptised.

It is a principle that is in Christian baptism as it was in the baptism of John unto repentance.

Baptism in itself does not wash away sins and was never intended to do so. The Apostle Peter makes this truth known in his letter,

"The like figure whereunto even baptism doth also now save us (not the putting away of the filth of the flesh, but the answer of a good conscience toward God,) by the resurrection of Jesus Christ" (1 Pe. 3:21).

Water baptism does not save you by cleansing your heart of sin, but rather is the outward response of a good conscience toward God by your obedience of faith (Rom. 16:26). That is why in instances where baptism is mentioned in Scripture, it relates to baptism with belief, repentance and conversion; and not baptism on its own (Ac. 2:38; 8:12, 36-38; 9:17-18; 10:46-48; 19:1-5). People who responded to the gospel first repented so that they might believe and then were baptised (Matt. 21:31-32; Mk. 1:14-15). Any who believe without repenting, his faith is not genuine, saving faith, but mere intellectual assent (Ja. 2:17-26).

In typology, we can see how water baptism is represented in the Old Testament; for example, the flood of Noah that destroyed the ungodly world, at the same time, saved Noah and his family who were in the ark, being lifted and carried by the water. And so in like manner, water baptism also saves us. As the water itself did not save Noah and his family, water baptism does not save us. However, by faith Noah prepared and built an ark for the saving of his family, thus becoming the heir of righteousness by faith according to Hebrews 11:7. The ark was the visible expression of Noah's faith in God, so when the flood waters came, it saved Noah and his family from the wicked influence of ungodly men and women in the world by destroying them (2 Pe. 2:5). While the flood waters were destruction to the ungodly, were salvation to the righteous.

In the same vein, water baptism saves us from the ungodly influence of the world, by virtue of our faith and obedience. Just to reiterate the words of Jesus, "He that believeth and is baptized shall be saved..." (Mk. 16:16). Faith with baptism saves you from Satan's counterattack to pull you back into sin and the ungodly influences of the world. This figurative picture of Christian baptism can also be seen in Israel's deliverance from Egyptian bondage. God by Moses brought Israel out of Egypt and headed towards the Red Sea. Pharaoh and his Egyptian army on chariots drawn by horses, pursued after Israel to the Red Sea. Moses, by the command and power of the Lord, divided the Red Sea making a dry path for the children of Israel to walk through (Ex. 14). The Apostle Paul describes this event that Israel was baptised in the cloud and in the sea (1 Cor. 10:1-2).

The Egyptian army pursued after them in the sea and God caused their chariot wheels to fall off so that they drove them heavily on the ground (Ex. 14:25). Then God commanded Moses to stretch forth his hand and the sea came together again drowning the Egyptians (v26-28). Israel's passage through the Red Sea was their baptism unto Moses. The Bible declares,

"By faith they passed through the Red sea as by dry land which the Egyptians assaying to do were drowned" (Heb. 11:29 NKJV).

By faith Israel was baptised in the Red Sea and were delivered by water from their Egyptian oppressors. However, the Egyptians, without faith, attempted to do so and were drowned. The Red Sea experience saved Israel from Pharaoh's counterattack to subdue them. Like the Egyptians, any person who is baptised without genuine repentance and faith in Jesus Christ will perish (Jn. 3:16, 34).

A third Old Testament picture of Christian baptism is the story of Naaman, a Syrian captain who was a leper (2 Kgs. 5:1-14). The king of Syria sent Naaman to Israel to be healed of his leprosy. After going to the king of Israel, he was sent to the Prophet Elisha, who commanded him to go and dip himself seven times in the River Jordan and he would be cured of his leprosy. He refused to obey the prophet, nevertheless, his servants eventually persuaded him to go, so he went, dipped himself seven times in the River Jordan and was healed of his leprosy. The River Jordan had no medicinal qualities of itself, it was Naaman's obedience to the word of the prophet that saved him from his leprosy. In like manner, it is not the baptismal water that saves, but rather our obedience to the Word of God to baptise.

The Early Church, in the book of Acts, fulfilled the Great Commission with respect to baptism, baptising people in the Name of Jesus (Ac. 2:38, 41; 8:12, 16; 10:47-48; 19:5). Since the book of Acts records that the apostles baptised in the Name of Jesus Christ, we must understand why the apostles did so, and how you reconcile the apparent contradiction of Matthew 28:19 to baptise in the Name of the Father, and of the Son and of the Holy Ghost.

The Epistles show that to baptise in the Name of Jesus signifies one's baptism into Jesus Christ for the name stands for the person. Also, baptism in that Name represents the believers identification and participation in the death, burial and resurrection of Jesus Christ (Rom. 6:3-5; Gal. 3:27; 5:24; Col. 2:12). Additionally, baptism in the Name of Jesus represents that Jesus Christ was crucified for us as implied in the Apostle Paul's statement in 2 Corinthians 1:13:

"Is Christ divided? Was Paul crucified for you? Or were ye baptized in the name of Paul?"

Paul's words suggest that the Corinthian brethren were baptised in the name of Jesus, with the understanding that Jesus Christ was crucified for them. Lastly, baptism in the Name of Jesus depicts the delegation of His authority to the believer whether doing or receiving baptism. John's Gospel declares,

"But as many as received Him, to them He gave the [authority] to become children of God, to those who believe in His <u>name</u>" (Jn. 1:12 NKJV).

The authority of Jesus in His death on the cross stripped Satan and his cohorts of all authority and we are all partakers of that authority through His Name. When He died, we died in Him, stripping the satanic foes and ruling over them in Christ (Col. 2:14-15; Heb. 2:14-15). Everything that Jesus did at the cross has been charged to our account as if we personally defeated the Devil. In Jesus' Name, the believer lives in His victory (2 Cor. 2:14).

Now the apostles heard the commission of Jesus to go and baptise in the Name of the Father, and of the Son, and of the Holy Ghost (Matt. 28:19). Why then, did they go and baptise in the Name of Jesus? To understand how to reconcile the two, you must know that (a) what Jesus said and (b) how the apostles carried it out, are not contradictions. The answer to this lies in the letter to the Colossians:

"In him dwelleth all the fullness of the Godhead bodily" (Col. 2:9).

The term "Godhead" is from the Greek rendering "theotes", meaning to be in the state of God, that is, to have the Divine nature and essence of God. Therefore Jesus was God incarnate in flesh (Jn. 1:1, 14). Moreover, in Him dwelt all fullness of Divinity. Knowing this, you come to understand that to baptise into Jesus Christ is to baptise into the triune God because the triune God dwells in Him, All of the Father, Son and Holy Spirit dwells in Jesus. He is the means by which we have communion with the triune God. Through baptism into the Name of Jesus, we are baptised into the Godhead.

6

The Baptism with the Holy Spirit

"And, being assembled together with them, commanded them that they should not depart from Jerusalem, but wait for the promise of the Father, which, saith he, ye have heard of me. For John truly baptized with water; but ye shall be baptized with the Holy Ghost not many days hence" (Ac. 1:4-5).

After the accomplishment of the work of redemption at the cross, Jesus is raised from death and is with His disciples about forty days, teaching them the things concerning the Kingdom of God. Before His ascension to heaven, Jesus gave strict instruction for His disciples to stay in Jerusalem and wait for the promise of the Father. That promise is defined in the following verse to be the baptism with the Holy Spirit. John the Baptist stated in his ministry what Jesus would come to do:

"I indeed baptize you with water unto repentance: but he that cometh after me is mightier than I, whose shoes I am not worthy

The Baptism with the Holy Spirit

to bear: he shall baptize you with the Holy Ghost and with fire" (Matt. 3:11).

John's statement concerning the purpose of Jesus' coming was so important that it is mentioned in all four Gospels: which is, to baptise with the Holy Spirit (Mk. 1:8; Lk. 3:16; Jn. 1:33). In this account, repentance is recorded in only three of the Gospels (Matt. 3:2, 8, 11; Mk. 1:4; Lk. 3:3, 8), and Christ being the Lamb of God who takes away the sin of the world is mentioned in John's Gospel only (Jn. 1:29, 36). The amount of times the subjects concerned occur in the Gospels teach how the sacrifice of Jesus, the Lamb of God, and the doctrine of repentance are to cleanse and resolve the sin problem as a means to a greater end: namely, the Baptism with the Holy Spirit. The sacrificial death of Jesus Christ paved the way for this experience to come to every Christian believer. God's actual intention was never to dwell in temples made with hands (Ac. 7:48-50) but to dwell in His redeemed people. That is why Jesus came to die on a cross to make this possible.

The baptism with the Holy Spirit is the indwelling fullness, presence and power of the Holy Spirit to overflowing; the manifestation of God in power and wisdom in the believer. Jesus stated that there would be a transition in regards to the coming of the Holy Spirit. He said,

"And I will pray the Father, and he shall give you another comforter, that he may abide with you for ever; even the Spirit of truth; whom the world cannot receive, because it seeth him not, neither knoweth him: but ye know him; for he dwelleth with you, and shall be in you" (Jn. 14:16-17).

In Jesus' last moments with His disciples before His crucifixion and death, he expounds unto them deep truths about the Godhead, the ministry and Person of Holy Spirit, who was about to come in a new way unlike the Old Testament dispensation (Jn. 7:37-39). Jesus declares His ministry in the Godhead as an intercessor: to pray to the Father to send the Holy Spirit. The Father is the Source and initiator from whom the work of the Godhead begins, and the Son receives the promise of the Spirt and directly sends Him from the father to the believer (Jn. 14:26; 15:26; 16:7). And the Holy Spirit Himself comes to dwell in the believer (1 Cor. 3:16; 6:19).

In above verses, Jesus calls the Holy Spirit "another comforter." This phrase reveals several things about the Holy Spirit. Firstly, the term in the Greek is "allos parakletos". "Allos" denotes - another of the same kind. As Jesus was a comforter to His disciples, the Holy Spirit would be another comforter just like Jesus in nature, character and ministry. While Jesus was God in the flesh, the Holy Spirit is God in Spirit, possessing the same moral and spiritual attributes as Jesus. Secondly, the Holy Spirit is a personality who is referred to, by Jesus, with masculine pronouns: He, Him, Himself. He speaks, hears, teaches, testifies and brings things to your remembrance (Jn. 14:26; 15:26; 16:7-13). The Greek rendering for comforter, "parakletos", literally means, one called alongside to help, and the synonyms for parakletos are advocate, helper, intercessor, counsellor, strengthener and standby.

Jesus calls the Holy Spirit "the Spirit of truth", whom the world cannot receive because it operates on the principle of sensory perception. On account of not knowing Jesus, the world does not know the Holy Spirit, except Jesus' disciples. For this reason,

The Baptism with the Holy Spirit

Jesus said, "... he dwelleth with you and shall be in you" (Jn. 14:17). He makes a distinction between the Holy Spirit being with you and dwelling in you. When he spoke these words to His disciples, he was making a distinction between the present and the future. As His disciples, they knew the Holy Spirit for He was with them, who revealed to them that Jesus was the Son of God; they were born again and in the Kingdom; they were clean by the Word Jesus had spoken unto them (Jn. 15:3). Jesus told them that the time was coming when the Holy Spirit would be dwelling in them. That time He referred to was the Day of Pentecost when they would be baptised in the Holy Spirit (Ac. 1:4-5; 2:1-4).

The disciples were saved and set apart from the world (Jn. 17:6, 8-15); Jesus stated in His prayer that they were not of the world, even as he was not of the world. They possessed divine knowledge of the Father and His Son (Jn. 17:3); Hence, the Spirit was with them, and so the Lord was about to go to the cross and pave the way for the Holy Spirit to come and inhabit His disciples. Jesus defined the baptism with the Holy Spirit to His disciples as receiving power in Acts 1:8,

"But ye shall receive power, after that the Holy Ghost is come upon you: and ye shall be witnesses unto me both in Jerusalem, and in all Judea, and in Samaria, and unto the uttermost part of the earth."

The Baptism with the Holy Spirit is a reception of power because the Holy Spirit coming upon them is the Source and Agent of that divine power. In the verse above, its purpose is to be a witness in preaching and to demonstrate with signs, wonders and miracles, to do supernaturally what could not be done in their own natural ability. This power is not only for witnessing but also to live as Jesus lived (1 Jn. 2:6) which requires us to walk in the Spirit so that we do not fulfil the lusts of the flesh (Gal. 5:16). Living the successful Christian life is impossible without the baptism with the Holy Spirit. He empowers us to bring forth the new life that we received when we were born again (Rom. 6:4; Titus 3:5).

The book of Acts shows us how the Holy Spirit was given, as well as and what signified receipt of this empowerment. In Acts 2:1-4, the Holy Spirit came upon the believers as a rushing mighty wind, and with tongues of fire that sat upon each of them. The account follows on,

"And they were all filled with the Holy Ghost, and began to speak with other tongues, as the Spirit gave them utterance" (v4).

Another term for the baptism with the Holy Ghost is being filled with the Holy Ghost; both terms are used interchangeably. They were filled to overflowing and began to speak in other tongues as the Spirit gave them utterance. The sign is that they spoke supernaturally in other tongues – tongues, meaning true languages. They spoke in languages they did not learn because they came from the Holy Spirit (v4). All the people who were present heard them speak in their own tongue (v7-11). They being uncertain of what the sign meant, some supposing that these men were drunk with wine, Peter stood up and preached his sermon from the Joel 2:28-32, concluding that Jesus Christ has been exalted, receiving of the Father the promise of the Spirit, he has poured forth this which they now see and hear (v33). Thus, the baptism with the Holy Spirit was accompanied by what they saw and heard. There was evidence; they saw and heard them speak in tongues.

In Acts 8:14, the apostles at Jerusalem heard that the Samaritans had received the Word of God. How did they receive it? They believed the Word that Philip preached and were baptised (v12). And so the apostles sent Peter and John to Samaria. When they had come, the Bible declares,

"Who, when they were come down, prayed for them, that they might receive the Holy Ghost: (For as yet he was fallen upon none of them: only they were baptized in the name of the Lord Jesus)" (v16).

This verse presents the distinction between salvation and the baptism with the Holy Spirit, as subsequent to the new birth. The receiving of the Word is the new birth because we are born again of the Word (1 Pe. 1:23). They believed and responded by being baptised, which confirms that they were saved (Mk. 16:16). "Receiving the Holy Ghost" or "the Holy Ghost falling on them" are clauses that allude to the baptism with the Holy Ghost. The passage goes on to state,

"Then laid they their hands on them, and they received the Holy Ghost. And when Simon saw that through the laying on of the apostles' hands the Holy Ghost was given, he offered them money, Saying, Give me also this power that on whomsoever I lay hands, he may receive the Holy Ghost" (v17-18).

When the apostles laid their hands on the Samaritans, they received the Holy Spirit with the accompaniment of visible evidence, for verse 18 states that Simon saw that by the laying on of the apostles' hands, the Holy Spirit was given, and therefore offered them money. Simon saw evidence of the Samaritans receiving the Holy Spirit. That evidence is what the Jewish pilgrims saw and heard: namely, speaking in tongues (Ac. 2:4, 7-11, 33). This experience is defined by the Apostle Peter as the gift of God (v19).

Take note in Acts 10, of how the Gentiles received the Holy Spirit. Consequently, the sovereignty and providence of God brought together, Peter and Cornelius - the Roman centurion, along with his household. The apostle preached unto them and while he was speaking, the Holy Spirit fell upon those who heard the Word (v34-44), and the biblical narrative follows on,

"And they of the circumcision which believed were astonished, as many as came with Peter, because that on the Gentiles also was poured out the gift of the Holy Ghost. For they heard them speak with tongues, and magnified God..." (Ac. 10:45-46).

The Jewish believers knew that the gift of the Holy Spirit was poured out upon the Gentiles, also described as the Holy Ghost falling upon them, was because they heard them speak with tongues (v46), and Peter concluded by saying in verse 47,

"Can any man forbid water, that these should not be baptized, which have received the Holy Ghost as well as we?"

Peter identifies the Gentiles' experience of the Holy Spirit to be tantamount to his experience on the Day of Pentecost (Ac. 2:1-4; 11:15-17). The same evidence or sign of speaking in tongues in Acts 2 is also seen and heard among the Gentiles in Acts 10. It brought about a greater understanding to the Jews, of the Plan of salvation for the Gentiles. Moreover, they understood that God had granted to the Gentiles, repentance unto life (Ac. 11:18). In this instance, Cornelius and those who were with him received two distinct experiences together: repentance unto salvation (2 Cor. 7:10), and the baptism with the Holy Spirit – the seal of their redemption (2 Cor. 1:21-22; Eph. 1:13-14; 4:30).

Another example of the Holy Spirit outpouring is among the disciples of John in Acts 19:1-6. The Apostle Paul went down to Ephesus, found certain disciples, and assuming they were Christian believers asked,

"...Have ye received the Holy Ghost since ye believed?..." (Ac. 19:2).

I want you to stop here for a moment to ponder what Paul is asking, because it is showing that it is possible to be a believer and not have received the Holy Spirit, or else Paul would not have asked the question. Anyone who believes automatically receives eternal life (Jn. 3:16, 18; 2 Thess. 2:13). But the baptism with the Holy Spirit is a separate experience subsequent to salvation. Paul, in his own mind sees them as two distinct experiences. Paul's continued discourse with them reveals that they are disciples of John the Baptist and expounds to them that John was a foreunner of Jesus Christ (v2-4). They received the message and were baptised in the Name of the Lord Jesus (v5). The passage of scripture follows on,

"And when Paul had laid his hands upon them, the Holy Ghost came on them; and they spake with tongues, and prophesied" (Ac. 19:6).

Here we see again speaking in tongues, as the initial sign of the baptism with the Holy Spirit.

One of the principles of correct biblical interpretation is that in the mouth of two or three witnesses, let every word be established (Deut. 17:6; Matt. 18:16). I have given you three definite, scriptural witnesses that speaking in tongues is the initial sign of the baptism with the Holy Spirit (e.g. Ac. 2:1-4; 10:46-47; 19:6), and Acts 8:18 is based contextually on the previous three. And prior to the coming of the Holy Spirit, Jesus stated in His commission that believers, in His Name, would speak with new tongues (Mk. 16:17).

God chose speaking in tongues as a sign of the baptism with the Holy Spirit rather than the unreliable fleeting emotions that fluctuate dependant on one's experiences of life. Since a person experiences the joy of salvation at the new birth, he would need something additional or more concrete as confirmation of a subsequent experience. And so God has chosen speaking in tongues for four reasons:

1) supernatural evidence: speaking supernaturally a language you did not learn
2) universal evidence: it is a sign that is not an isolated incident, but is seen every place where the baptism with the Holy Spirit is experienced
3) outward evidence: speaking in tongues is an utterance that can be seen and heard by others
4) uniform evidence: every time a group of people received the baptism with the Holy Spirit in the book of Acts, it was invariably accompanied by speaking in tongues.

How to Receive the Baptism with the Holy

Spirit

Here are several biblical principles of how to receive the Holy Spirit with the evidence of speaking in tongues:

1) Ground your faith in this scriptural promise based on the Word of God for faith comes by hearing and hearing by the Word of God (Rom. 10:17; Ac. 2:16-18, 38-39; Gal. 3:2)
2) Ask the Father in prayer for the gift of the Holy Spirit (Lk. 11:13; Jn. 15:16; 16:23)
3) Believe that you receive when you pray (Mk. 11:24; 1 Jn. 5:14-15)
4) Act your faith by speaking forth from your spirit, not your head, the utterances of the Holy Spirit (Ps. 81:10; Ac. 2:1-4; 2 Cor. 4: 13; Ja. 2:14-26).

7

Speaking in Tongues

"For he that speaketh in an unknown tongue speaketh not unto men, but unto God; for no man understandeth him; howbeit in the spirit he speaketh mysteries" (1 Cor. 14:2).

In the previous chapter, I dealt with speaking in tongues as the initial evidence of the baptism with the Holy Spirit. For this chapter, I want to discuss the value and benefits of speaking with tongues in the personal life of a Spirit-filled believer. Speaking in tongues does have its public use as communicated by the Apostle Paul in 1 Corinthians 14, but that is not the focus of this discussion. However, Paul does mention its personal use and benefit, and exhorts believers to continue speaking in tongues (1 Cor. 14:4, 28, 39).

To remind you of the definition of tongues, it is speaking supernaturally by the Spirit, a true language not learned or understood by the speaker. The Apostle Paul alludes to this fact by saying,

"For if I pray in an unknown tongue, my spirit prayeth, but my understanding is unfruitful. What is it then? I will pray with the spirit, and I will pray with the understanding also..." (1 Cor. 14:14-15a).

Paul relates speaking in tongues to the ministry of prayer and prayer is talking to God. Therefore when one prays in tongues, one is not speaking to men but to God. To reiterate the opening verse of this chapter,

"For he that speaketh in an unknown tongue speaketh not unto men, but unto God; for no man understandeth him; howbeit in the spirit he speaketh mysteries" (1 Cor. 14:2).

There are two kinds of prayers referred to in verse 15: praying with the spirit, and praying with the understanding. Both are never confused or used interchangeably in Scripture. The Apostle Paul lays down the terms for both and their respective meanings. Praying with the spirit (v14-16) or in the spirit (v2) are both referring to praying in tongues and praying with the understanding is praying in a language that you understand. The former is known in Pentecostal circles as praying in the spirit. So when one prays in tongues, his spirit is praying while his understanding is unfruitful (v14).

Now, the apostle Paul shows us how a Spirit-filled person can activate their supernatural prayer language in verse 15:

"...I will pray with the spirit, and I will pray with the understanding also."

You activate your supernatural prayer language by an act of your will in the same way you would choose to pray with your understanding. You may ask, 'How is this Scriptural'? Because the Holy Spirit is always in you (Jn. 14:17), therefore, you can choose to speak in tongues at any time you so desire for the Holy Spirit is always available to give you utterance (Ac. 2:4). In addition, the reason why you can speak in tongues at any time is because your faith is not a moment in time, but a lifestyle. The Bible states,

"For therein is the righteousness of God revealed from faith to faith: as it is written, The just shall live by faith" (Rom. 1:17).

I can activate my prayer language at any time, whether I feel like it or not, whether I am at church or walking on the streets. Faith's presence in your human spirit can be exercised regardless of your circumstances, simply because faith is a law that can activate this gift at any time (Rom. 3:27).

Every Spirit-filled believer is instructed in the New Testament to pray in the spirit, that is, in tongues (1 Cor. 14:2, 14-15). In the spiritual warfare passage of Ephesians 6:18, it declares,

"praying always with all prayer and supplication in the Spirit, and watching thereunto with all perseverance and supplication for all saints."

First of all, the Apostle Paul exhorts us to pray always. That term "always" is from the Greek: 2en panti kairo", meaning in every season, time, opportunity and occasion. We are instructed to pray with all kinds of prayer and supplication in the Spirit. Just as you pray with your understanding at every opportunity and occasion, you should also, at every opportunity, pray in tongues and build up your spirit. The Apostle Paul practised what he preached. He said,

"I thank my God, I speak with tongues more than ye all" (1 Cor. 14:18).

The brethren whom Paul was addressing were avid and excessive tongue speakers, to the extent that Paul had to give them some regulations on its use in the public assembly (1 Cor. 14:27-29) and yet, he said that he spoke in tongues more than them. How could this be possible given the fact that he would rather speak five words with his understanding than ten thousand words in an unknown tongue (v18)? The answer is, he did much of his praying with tongues in his private prayer time, an example for every Spirit-filled person to follow.

Now, I want to answer the question as to why it is important and beneficial for a believer to pray in tongues. Paul states in his letter to the Corinthians:

"He that speaketh in an unknown tongue edifieth himself..." (14:4a).

The verb "edifieth" is from the Greek rendering: "oikodomeo", which literally means to build a house, and is used figuratively and spiritually for the promotion of spiritual progress, growth and development of character (Ac. 9:31; 1 Thess. 5:11). Spending long periods of time praying in tongues will enhance and speed up your spiritual progress and growth to a greater extent than praying with your understanding only. Speaking in tongues will enable you to take giant steps in the realm of the Spirit. It is like a battery charger or power generator. By the baptism with the Holy Spirit, the power comes to reside within you (Ac. 1:8), but through praying in tongues, you generate that power to work on your behalf, building you up spiritually to accomplish your Kingdom assignment. Speaking in tongues will keep you charged up.

The Apostle Paul encouraged Timothy:

"Wherefore I put thee in remembrance that thou stir up the gift of God, which is in thee by the putting on of my hands" (2 Tim. 1:6).

The term "stir up" is from the Greek word "anazopureo", which signifies to kindle afresh, or to keep in full flame. This alludes to the fact that the gift of God in you can diminish in potency as a result of neglect or lack of use (1 Tim. 4:14). Praying in tongues is the fastest way of igniting, inflaming and recharging your human spirit. That is why Jude instructs the brethren,

"but ye, beloved, building up yourselves on your most holy faith, praying in the Holy Ghost" (1:20).

The word "building" in the Greek is akin to the term "edify" used with reference to praying in tongues (1 Cor. 14:4). Therefore, Jude alluding to the same experience, instructs us to build ourselves up on our most holy faith by praying in the Holy Spirit. When praying in the Spirit, you edify and build up yourself spiritually; you grow up, become emboldened and your spirit is strengthened to do God's Will. These spiritual benefits do not happen separately from God's Word. We are to build ourselves on our most holy faith and faith is predicated by God's Word, because faith comes by hearing the Word of God (Rom. 10:17). As you study the Word, praying in tongues will drive the Word deep within your heart to establish and strengthen you. The faith based on the Word of God must be resident in you if it is to be strengthened by praying in tongues. Faith must be the foundation upon which you pray in the Spirit.

Praying in the Holy Spirt presents another dimension to praying in tongues. It is not just your spirit praying but the Holy Spirit is praying in you and through you to the Father. The Bible informs us,

"Likewise the Spirt also helpeth our infirmities: for we know not what we should pray for as we ought: but the Spirit maketh intercession for us with groanings which cannot be uttered. And he that searcheth the hearts knoweth what is the mind of the Spirit, because he maketh intercession for the saints according to the will of God" (Rom. 8:26-27).

According to this passage of scripture, there are three essential aspects to the prayer ministry of the Holy Spirit: firstly, he helps us in our weaknesses; secondly, He makes intercession for us; and thirdly, He makes intercession for the saints according to the Will of God. Understanding that the Holy Spirit is the Subject of both verses is key to interpreting this passage correctly. Let us therefore begin to examine these three important features of the Holy Spirit's prayer ministry in the believer.

First, the Holy Spirit helps us in our weaknesses. The term "helpeth" is from the Greek rendering: "sunantilambano", and it literally means to take hold together with. Its idea is not of taking a burden for someone, but rather of one taking hold of a burden together with, and thus, lightening the load of another. The Holy Spirit, through the ministry of prayer takes hold together with us in our infirmities or weaknesses. He helps us when we do not know what to pray or how to pray as we should. But the Holy Spirit Himself will make intercession for us by praying together with us. The notion here is not of the Spirit teaching you how to pray but rather He Himself making intercession in the believer and for the believer, when he is ignorant of what or how to pray. Ignorance is a weakness that the Spirit has come to help us with. Intercession refers to praying on behalf of someone else, therefore, the Spirit's prayer ministry on behalf of believers is an intercessory ministry: - "...he maketh intercession for the saints..."

Next, how does He intercede? Before answering that question, the New Testament shows us that the Spirit dwells within us and so He intercedes in us (Jn. 14:17; Rom. 8:9; 1 Cor. 3:16); He intercedes with us (Rom. 8:26a) and also intercedes for us (Rom. 8:26b, 27b). Now, concerning how the Spirit intercedes, the Bible states,

"...but the Spirit itself maketh intercession for us with groanings which cannot be uttered" (Rom. 8:26b).

The Spirit Himself intercedes with groanings which cannot be uttered. The clause: "groanings which cannot be uttered" is from the Greek: "steagmois alaletois", which denotes unutterable groans or sighs that cannot be put into words; the reason is - we do not know what or how to pray as we ought. But the Holy Spirit Himself will intercede, putting a language of utterance to those inexpressible groanings, thus enabling the believer to pray forth those groanings in a language of the Spirit according to the

Speaking in Tongues

will of God. That language referred to, is speaking in tongues. The believer speaks and the Spirit gives him utterance (Ac. 2:4). This prayer in the Spirit removes all barriers of ignorance in prayer where you will be praying one hundred percent according to the will of God. Verse 27 of Romans 8 states that the Holy Spirit makes intercession for the saints according to the will of God.

The next verse (v27) states, "he that searcheth the hearts..." The "he" of this clause is reiterating the subject of the previous verse: the Holy Spirit. In grammatical construction, the pronouns he, she or it are used to refer to the subject noun of the preceding sentence. In this context the pronoun is alluding to the Holy Spirit because this is what the Apostle Paul is referring to. The Holy Spirit searches, or, in other words, knows the hearts of men. The adjacent clause also says that He knows the mind of the Spirit. The phrase "mind of the spirit" here is not alluding to the Holy Spirit, but rather refers to the mind of the recreated human spirit in the believer (see 1 Cor. 2:11; Eph. 4:23). In verse 6 of Romans 8, the term "mind of the spirit" is mentioned in the original Greek language, but the translator conveyed the sense of that verse in English as to be "spiritually minded". And so the Holy Spirit knows what is in the mind of the recreated human spirit because He makes intercession for the saints according to the will of God.

There are seven specific benefits to praying in tongues:

- defeating the weakness of not knowing how to pray (Rom. 8:26-27)
- it is a tool that will help you to endure and overcome temptation (Matt. 26:41a;1 Cor. 10:13; Heb. 4:15)

- speaking in tongues will open your understanding to the deeper mysteries of God's Word (Jn. 16:12-13; 1 Cor. 2:9-10)
- producing confidence and boldness (2 Tim. 1:6-7); praying in tongues gives spiritual rest and refreshing (Isa. 28:11-12; 1 Cor. 14:21-22)
- unfolding the hidden counsel of God for your life (Prov. 20:5; Jn. 7:37-39)
- strengthening your faith in God's Word (Jude 1:20)
- ehancing your sensitivity to the leading and direction of the Spirit (Rom. 8:14, 16).

As you spend time praying in tongues on a daily basis, you see a positive difference and growth in your life. It will charge you up spiritually to walk the Christian life in the power of God and not in your own strength (Gal. 5:16, 22-23). Stir up yourself by speaking in tongues and let the Holy Spirit to have the ascendancy in your life.

8

Lord, Teach Us to Pray

"And it came to pass, that, as he was praying in a certain place, when he ceased, one of his disciples said unto him, Lord, teach us to pray, as John also taught his disciples" (Lk. 11:1).

Jesus' life was saturated and replete with prayer to the extent that one of His disciples asked Him to teach them to pray. This type of prayer is referring to praying with your understanding because you can teach someone what to say when they pray, but cannot teach someone what to say in tongues since it is an utterance that comes by the Spirit (Ac. 2:4; 1 Cor. 14:14). Additionally, this request that was made by one of Jesus' disciples was prior to the outpouring of the Spirit at Pentecost (Ac. 2:1-4). So this chapter will be dealing with how to pray with understanding that is in harmony with God's Word.

When Jesus' disciple asked Him to teach them to pray, He did not teach them to recite a prayer. but rather gave them a model –

a pattern and example on what and how to pray that would relate to their whole life of prayer. In this model, Jesus taught the essential principles of prayer for His disciples to use in their own prayer time with God. His primary intention was for His disciples to understand the principles He taught and put them into practice. There are several principles in the Lord's Prayer I want to cover that will make your own prayer life effective.

In Luke 11:2-4, Jesus begins His teaching declaring, "When ye pray, say..." The first principle He teaches is that when you pray, say – that is, open your mouth and utter words to God; speak with your mouth. God has ordained life and strength in the practice of speaking with the mouth (Ps. 8:2; Prov. 18:20-21). Every person who prayed to God in the Bible said with the mouth (1 Sam. 1:10-17; Jn. 11:41-43). In addition, the most natural means of communication is with the mouth. Friendships are nurtured, cultivated and developed through verbal communication. When verbal communication is lacking in a relationship, it will suffer. In like manner, if you do not speak to the Father in prayer, your relationship with Him will suffer.

Jesus went on further to say, "Our Father..." (v2). The second principle that Jesus taught is that prayer is talking to Father God. Biblical prayer is not speaking to devils; when you speak to devils, you should be commanding them to come out of people. When praying the Bible way, you should be praying exclusively to God (Matt. 26:39-43; Jn. 15:16; 16:23-24), not saints, devils or angels.

Now, regarding the content of the Lord's Prayer, the first part of the prayer (v2) is a God-centred declaration; the last part of that prayer is a human-centred petition (v3-4). The mainspring of our prayer should be first and foremost God focused and our declaration of Him should be our protocol of relating with Him prior to our petitions.

Jesus taught that we should address God as our Father. In this, He teaches us the principle of relationship through the new birth (Jn. 3:3-6; 1 Jn. 3:1). Prayer's primary purpose is relationship; petitioning is secondary. Relationship with God should be the focal point of your prayer – spending quality time getting to know the Father. This is the highest purpose in the divine, human experience in prayer. The Lord's Prayer unveils our divine sonship to the Father. Galatians 4:5-7 states that Jesus Christ came,

"To redeem them that were under the law, that we might receive the adoption of sons. And because ye are sons, God hath sent forth the Spirit of his Son into your hearts, crying, Abba Father. Wherefore thou art no more a servant, but a son; and if a son, then an heir of God through Christ."

Calling God our Father testifies to the fact that we have received the adoption of sons, and as sons we have been given rights, privileges, authority, inheritance and blessings. We now have the authority to call God Father. God as our Father implies several things from Scripture: He will answer every request that we ask of Him (Jn. 15:7, 16); he will give good gifts to His children who ask Him (Matt. 7:9-11; Lk. 11:11-13); He desires to have a close relationship with His children (Jn. 14:16-18, 23; Gal. 4:6; Rom. 8:15); and as Father, He will be our counsellor, guide and teacher (Jn. 14:26; 16:13-14). Therefore, pray to your Father with a consciousness of sonship, not with a sense of inferiority. The Bible says that we are to come boldly to the throne of grace that we may obtain mercy and find grace to help in time of need (Heb. 4:16).

Jesus, then, says in His prayer, "Hallowed be thy name." this clause conveys two principles: 1) a recognition of His holiness and 2) a declaration of praise. Hallowed is from the Greek word "hagiazo", which signifies to make holy, to sanctify or set apart. It is used in the clause, in the passive. The idea here is not of making God holy, as if he was not already holy, but the usage in its true biblical context is to recognise and regard Him as holy, separating Him from everything that is common. Every living and finite thing has something in common: we were all created whereas God is not created; he is the Creator without beginning. He is also separated from everything that is unclean for He is pure and righteous in His character and person which is what is meant by the word "name." So when we pray to Him, we must regard Him as holy. The Bible declares,

"...This is what the Lord spoke saying: "By those who come near Me I must be regarded as holy: And before all the people I must be glorified..." (Lev. 10:3 NKJV).

God's holiness – His separateness, otherness and greatness that positions Him far above all creation will strike awe and apprehension in the heart of a worshipper, demanding a response of reverence. This is how the Prophet Isaiah responded when he had a vision of the holiness of God (Is 6). Heaven is incessantly crying holy, holy, holy because His holiness is the constant focus of heaven (Is. 6:2-3; Rev. 4:8).

Jesus, in teaching us to pray, summarises the principle of praise by saying, "hallowed be thy name." Praise must be involved in our prayer time with the Father. The Bible teaches that God inhabits the praises of His people (Ps. 22:3. It gives God pleasure to see His people praise Him: declaring who He is and what He has done for us. It is speaking well of Him and giving Him thanks for His goodness to us (Ps. 107:21). This is blessing the Lord. We are encouraged in Scripture to bless the Lord with all of our soul and not forget His benefits towards us (Ps. 103:1-5). The psalmist announces,

"I will bless the LORD at all times: his praise shall continually be in my mouth" (Ps. 34:1).

Praise ought to be a lifestyle in the believer's walk with the Lord, when things are looking well and when things seem dire. The Scripture declares that in everything, we should give God thanks (1 Thess. 5:18). Why? Because praise has an effect on God, on you and on your spiritual adversaries. I have already said that God takes pleasure and delight in our praises and therefore will respond to us with blessings (Rev. 4:11). Then praise has an effect on you,

"And be not drunk with wine wherein is excess; but be filled with the Spirit; Speaking to yourselves in psalms and hymns and spiritual songs, singing and making melody in your heart to the Lord; Giving thanks always for all things unto God and the Father in the name of our Lord Jesus Christ" (Eph. 5:18-20).

This passage exhorts us not to be drunk with wine but to be filled with the Spirit. The next verses tell us how to do that: speaking to yourselves in psalms, hymns and spiritual songs to the Lord; giving thanks to Him for all things. The context is about praise and thanksgiving. When a believer perform these spiritual disciplines on a daily basis, he will be filled with the Spirit.

Lastly, the praise and thanksgiving of a believer will have an effect on His spiritual adversaries. Psalm 8:2 states,

"Out of the mouth of babes and sucklings hast thou ordained strength because of thine enemies that thou mightest still the enemy and the avenger."

God has ordained strength out of the mouth of babes and sucklings; a verse quoted by Jesus on the day of His triumphant entry into Jerusalem. His quote of the verse substituted the phrase "perfected praise" for "ordained strength" (Ps. 8:2; Matt. 21:16) which tells us that God has appointed strength out of the mouth of perfected praise because of our enemies, to stop or put them to silence. In other words praise and thanksgiving will stop the enemy in his tracks. Through praise, the Lord sent an ambush against Judah's enemies (2 Chron. 20). Praise will defeat Satan's attacks against us if we only learn to focus on Him through praise. It will greatly magnify your focus on God's mighty Name.

The next phrase of the Lord's Prayer says, "Thy kingdom come." The concept of the Kingdom of God was central to the Old and New Testaments. In the post-exilic period, God's people had a heightened expectation awaiting the coming kingdom on earth, through Messiah. However, when John the Baptist arrived, he came preaching that the Kingdom of God was here; many believed and pressed their way into it (Lk. 16:16; Matt. 11:12). Jesus also came preaching the same message (Mk. 1:15) - which was perpetuated by His followers (Matt. 10:7-8; Lk. 10:9) and will be the message of the last days prior to the Lord's imminent return (Matt. 24:14). But in the meantime, we are to pray, "Thy kingdom come, Thy will be done, as in heaven, so in earth" (v2). The Kingdom is the sphere of God's rule and reign. His perfect rule and reign is already established in heaven, where God's perfect will is being done. Its by-product is that there is no sin, wars, hatred, famine, disease, rebellion, oppression or fear among heaven's citizens. And so every Bible believer is expecting God's Kingdom to be visibly established in the same manner on earth through Jesus Christ. However, at present there are wickedness, murders, crimes, diseases and catstrophies, demonic oppressions and addictions on earth. That is why we ought to pray for the Kingdom rule of God to intervene in these adverse events and circumstances.

The kingdom of darkness is prevalent in the earth with Satan at its head, who is described in Scripture to be the god of this world. But when God's people pray, His kingdom intervenes and changes the oppressive, adverse situations into peace, righteous and healthy reflections, signifying that God's Kingdom has come. Prayer will cause God's Kingdom to be manifested in the circumstance or person that has been prayed for. Things, circumstances and people are changed by the Kingdom through prayer. God's perfect rule in the earth functions through the prayers of His people. When they pray for all in authority (1 Tim. 2:1-2), for those who preach the gospel of the kingdom (Matt.9:37-10:1-8; Eph. 6:18-19) and for other dire situations that would hinder the progress of the Kingdom until the Lord returns to establish His visible Millennial Kingdom, where God's will shall be perfectly done on earth, as it is done in heaven.

"Thy will be done, as in heaven, so in earth" denotes the principle of praying according to God's will; an example and summary of all effectual prayers. St John 5:14-15 declares,

"And this is the confidence that we have in him, that, if we ask anything according to his will, he heareth us: And if we know that he hear us, whatsoever we ask, we know that we have the petitions that we desired of him."

The three ingredients of effectual prayer that stands out in this verse are: "confidence" (Gk boldness), "ask" and "know". Having confidence and boldness in God is based on your relationship with Him through Christ Jesus. Any sin or condemnation that interrupts that relationship will cause you to lose confidence (see 1 Jn. 3:21-22). We are to ask if we are to receive. James said, "...ye have not, because ye ask not" (4:2). God knows that you have needs but the way to appropriate them is by asking (Matt. 6:32; 7:7). Finally, we ought to know, and this knowing is based on the understanding of God's will. To know His will you must know His Word, for God's Word is a revelation of His will. Furthermore, putting His Word in your heart will give you the confidence to pray according to His will. Jesus said,

"If ye abide in me, and my words abide in you, ye shall ask what ye will, and it shall be done unto you" (Jn. 15:7).

Having a relationship with Jesus is through the Word abiding in you, and you shall ask whatever you will that is based on the Word, and it shall be given unto you.

The Lord's Prayer follows on to say, "Give us day by day our daily bread" (v3). This verse covers the whole financial realm of a believer; his physical sustenance such as food, drinks, clothing, money etc. God is concerned about our physical wellbeing as well as our spiritual, and he affirms that we should pray for our financial and physical wellbeing. Jesus explains this in greater detail in the Sermon on the Mount (Matt. 6:19-33). The comprehensive theme of the passage is summed up in verse 33,

"But seek ye first the kingdom of God, and his righteousness; and all these things shall be added unto you."

While you seek to do God's kingdom assignment and fulfil His righteous cause, He will take pleasure in prospering financially, His servants (Ps. 35:27). He is willing to supply all your needs according to His riches in glory by Christ Jesus (Phil. 4:19). What we need, we are to appropriate by asking with the right attitude. There are several things you need to bear in mind that identify the right attitude: 1) do not be covetous about material possessions for it is idolatry (Matt. 6:19-24; Col. 3:5); 2) do not be anxious about what you need but cast them, by prayer, upon the Lord (Matt. 6:25, 27-28; Phil. 4:5; 1 Pe 5:7); 3) doubt not but believe that God will supply your needs (Matt. 6:30; 21:22; Mk. 11:24; Phil. 4:19); 4) thank God for answering your request before you see the manifestation of the answer (Phil. 4:5; Mk. 11:24).

Then Jesus says in His teaching on prayer: "And forgive us our sins; for we also forgive every one that is indebted to us..." (v4). This is the principle of relationships void of offence, as it relates to prayer. There are two aspects to a Christian's relationship: the first clause of the verse refers to one's relationship with the One to whom he is praying, namely God. The second clause of the verse speaks to your relationship with your fellowman. The verse unveils the solution of how to remove an offence from your relationship with God.

Offences through unforgiveness will hinder your relationship with God. To have a clear channel of communication with God, you must forgive men their trespasses against you.

The way you relate to your neighbour is the way God will relate to you. God forgiving you will be dependent upon whether you forgive others. This principle of forgiveness is mentioned in other recorded passages of Christ's teachings (Matt. 6:12; 18:21-35; Mk. 11:25-26). Matthew 6:14-15 declares,

"For if ye forgive men their trespasses, your heavenly father will also forgive you: But if ye forgive not men their trespasses, neither will your heavenly Father forgive your trespasses."

A person who refuses to forgive, is one who has forgotten that he was forgiven. Therefore, the Apostle exhorts us saying,

"...if any man have a quarrel against any: even as Christ forgave you, so also do ye" (Col. 3:13).

So, as Jesus taught us that when we pray, we must forgive if we have something against someone, so that our heavenly Father may also forgive us our sins (Mk. 11:25-26). It is only the merciful who will obtain mercy (Matt. 5:7).

The Lord's Prayer concludes with this statement: And lead us not into temptation; but deliver us from evil (v4). Jesus summarises the basic principle of spiritual warfare. The clause "...deliver us from evil" is not merely talking about delivering us from moral evil but rather in the Greek, refers to us being delivered from the evil one, who is Satan. We are in a battle against Satan and his cohorts who are seeking to lay traps for us and lure us into them, but when we pray our heavenly Father will deliver us from the temptations of the evil one. Jesus affirms this to His disciples the night of His betrayal:

"Watch and pray, that ye enter not into temptation..." (Matt. 26:41a).

The disciples did not heed the urgency to pray but slumbered and slept. Jesus prepared Himself through prayer for what was about to come, overcame the temptation not to suffer and die, and went to the cross. By so doing, he triumphed over principalities and powers (Col. 2:14-15).

The Lord allows temptation to befall those who refuse to yield to His will and pray. God hardened Pharaoh's heart (Ex. 14:40) because Pharaoh chose to harden his own heart (1 Sam. 6:6). Those who pray with a true and humble heart invoke God's grace and mercy that will not give them over to the lusts of the flesh, but will deliver them from the evil one. Let us put on the armour of God so that we can stand against the wiles, deceits and trickeries of the Devil (Eph. 6:12).

9

How to Study the Bible

"**Study to shew thyself approved unto God, a workman that needeth not to be ashamed, rightly dividing the word of truth**" (2 Tim. 2:15).

Study should be central to the life of a disciple of Jesus Christ, since the term "disciple" in the Greek denotes a learner, student, pupil and scholar. Jesus affirms this by speaking to those Jews who believed in Him:

"...If ye continue in my word, then are ye my disciples indeed; And ye shall know the truth, and the truth shall make you free" (Jn. 8:31a-32).

Those Jews believed on Him but did not allow the word that He spoke to take residence in their hearts, therefore they remained in bondage to sin and were not aware of it (v33). Jesus clarified that He was talking about the bondage of sin, not physical slavery (v34). So, according to the context, Jesus was stating that if you continue, abide and remain in His Word, not allowing Satan to take the Word-seed that was sown in their hearts (Matt. 13:19; Mk. 4:15), they would know and understand the truth (Matt. 13:23), and the truth would make them free from the slavery of sin.

As it was important for you to receive the Word to become a true disciple of Jesus Christ, it will also be imperative to study the Word to be equipped, as a disciple, for every good work (2 Tim.3:16-17). To study the Bible effectively, you must take into account three important principles contained in the opening scripture (2 Tim. 2:15): 1) the motive of Bible study, 2) the purpose of Bible study, and 3) the manner of Bible study. These are the three areas I will be dealing with in this chapter.

THE MOTIVE

Motive deals with the reason why we do something and with respect to Bible study, it is important to study the Bible with the right motive, which is given in the opening clause of this verse of scripture: "Study to shew thyself approved unto God..." (2 Tim. 2:15). The Greek word for "study" is "spoudazo", which means diligence. It is first used in 2 Peter 1:10 to "...give diligence to make your calling and election sure...". It is also used in Hebrews 4:11 as "labour" – "let us labour therefore to enter into that rest...". The reason why we are to study the Bible is so that we can meet God's approval, not to be approved of men or to obtain self-approval. It is not for the purpose of showing people how much you know. The purpose of studying and giving diligence to the Word of God is so that we may know how to please God. The greatest enemy to a disciple of Jesus Christ is ignorance. Ignorance is destructive, but knowledge is empowering. The Prophet Hosea's resounding cry throughout the generations is this:

"My people are destroyed for lack of knowledge: because thou hast rejected knowledge, I will also reject thee, that thou shalt be no priest to me: seeing thou hast forgotten the law of thy God, I will also forget thy children" (Hos. 4:6).

This passage of scripture goes against a statement which states, "what you don't know won't hurt you". The scriptural reference shows us that what you do not know is destroying you. When you do not take every opportunity to learn the Word, Satan will take advantage of your ignorance and use it against you to destroy you. Studying God's Word with the right motive: to please Him, your life will improve, becoming better and stronger and you will live a complete and fulfilled life (Ac. 20:32; 1 Pe. 2:2).

Having the right motive and openness to please God will guide you to correctly handling the Word of God. Furthermore, it will cause you to approach the Word without ungodly preconceived ideas, biases and prejudice that would blind you to the plain truth. The Apostle Paul declares this when he said,

"But have renounced the hidden things of dishonesty, not walking in craftiness, nor handling the Word of God deceitfully; but by manifestation of the truth commending ourselves to every man's conscience in the sight of God" (2 Cor. 4:2).

The process is this, if you remove the hidden things of dishonesty from your heart, you will not handle the Word of God deceitfully. There are those who have unrighteous motives and agendas who pervert the Word of God to their own destruction, handling it deceitfully (2 Pe. 3:16). Never treat the Bible as an academic book to study intellectually, but treat it as sacred – God's holy Word.

Purpose

The purpose of Bible study is seen in the next clause: "...a workman that needeth not to be ashamed". In other words we are to study to become workers in the Kingdom of God; to be doers of the Word and not hearers only. The book of James states,

"But be ye doers of the word, and not hearers only, deceiving your own selves. For if any be a hearer of the word, and not a doer, he is like unto a man beholding his natural face in a glass: For he beholdeth himself, and goeth his way, and straightway forgetteth what manner of man he was" (Ja. 1:22-24).

Anyone who hears God's Word whether by personal study time whereby he hears it within himself, or hearing it taught to him, and does not practically apply the Word to his daily life, is deceiving himself. He is compared to a man beholding his natural face in a reflective mirror and immediately goes his way forgetting what manner of man he was.

In 2 Corinthians 3:18, the Word of God is also referred to in this passage as a mirror:

"but we all with open face beholding as in a glass the glory of the Lord, are changed into the same image from glory to glory, even as by the Spirit of the Lord."

The person who hears but does not obey has an irreverent attitude towards the Word. He looks at himself in the mirror of the Word but does not spend sufficient time in it, neither does he give the Word time to work in his heart for he looks in it and straight a way goes his way, forgetting what manner of man he was.

However, the person who hears and does the Word is described by James in this manner,

"But whoso looketh into the perfect law of liberty, and continueth therein, he being not a forgetful hearer, but a doer of the work, this man shall be blessed in his deeds" (Ja. 1:25).

This person looks continually into the mirror, the perfect law of liberty, and is not a forgetful hearer; he does not allow the things that he has learned to slip (Heb. 2:1). He lives in the Word day and night so that he becomes the Word written in his heart (Ps. 1:3; 2 Cor. 3:2-3). He persists with the Word long enough to change his thinking, his behaviour and his destiny. It is through consistency that we obtain the power to do the Word, because the seed of the Word is in us, therefore it is in our nature to be Word-practitioners (1Jn. 3:9).

There are two things the mirror of God's Word shows us: 1) what we really look like, and 2) what abnormalities exist that we need to remove. Firstly, as we are able to behold our natural face or image in a mirror, the Word of God is a mirror that unveils to us our true spiritual image, the face of our new birth (Jn. 3:3, 5), literally rendered in the original Greek, "face of his birth", (Ja. 1:23). I believe that doing the Word is inextricably linked to understanding and being reminded of your identity in Christ, and you maintain that identity-consciousness by the Word. Secondly, the Word as a spiritual mirror shows up any defects, blemishes or improprieties that need to be corrected. It is by the Word that we are washed and cleansed as we behold the glory of the Lord and are transformed into the same image from one level of glory to another (Jn. 15:3; 2 Cor. 3:18; Eph. 5:26-27).

THE MANNER

The manner of Bible study answers the question of how to study the Bible, and this is done by "...rightly dividing the word of truth" (2 Tim. 2:15). The phrase "rightly divided" is from the Greek word "orthotomeo", which literally means to cut straight. This was a sacrificial term used by Paul that referred to correctly cutting up a sacrificial animal into pieces and putting them in an orderly manner upon the altar according to certain rules (Edersheim 1994). Moreover, in the figurative sense when applied to the Word of truth, the meaning is of interpreting and teaching the Word of truth accurately and correctly according to the biblical rules of interpretation. There are specific rules of interpretation that you must follow with the guidance of the Holy Spirit. These rules will help you to interpret Scripture correctly.

Firstly, you must engage in an exegesis which is a systematic study of the Word of God to discover its original intended meaning. This involves studying a verse or passage of scripture according to its immediate context and remote context. Immediate context is taking into consideration what is preceded by a verse or passage of scripture and what comes after it. Secondly, remote context is looking at scripture in light of the whole biblical revelation. A scripture taken out of context will lead to erroneous notions and doctrines. It is said that a text out of context is a pretext. When looking at a text, consider who are the characters: who is speaking? And who is being spoken to? What are the circumstances surrounding the characters in the story? Also take into account the narrator's purpose for writing a story or book.

For example, in John 12:32 Jesus said,

"And I, if I be lifted up from the earth, will draw all men unto me."

This statement has been misinterpreted to mean lifting Jesus up or exalting Him through praise and worship. This interpretation may seem plausible when hearing or reading it in isolation, but the immediate context interprets the verse differently. The following verse explains what Jesus meant through the narrator,

"This he said, signifying what death he should die" (v33).

The Apostle John explains the statement to be referring to His method of death by crucifixion, a manner of humiliation, not exaltation. Another example is Psalm 2:7 which reads,

"I will declare the decree: the LORD hath said unto me, Thou art my Son; this day have I begotten thee."

From the plain surface of the text, it is possibly referring to the conception and birth of the Son of God if interpreted on its own. However, what I am about to explain is an example of interpreting scripture according to its remote context. The Apostle Paul in Acts 13:32-34a, teaches,

"And we declare unto you glad tidings, how that the promise which was made unto the fathers, God hath fulfilled the same unto us their children, in that he hath raised up Jesus again; as it is also written in the second psalm, Thou art my Son, this day have I begotten thee. And as concerning that he raised him up from the dead..."

The Apostle Paul explains verse 7 of the Messianic psalm to denote the bodily resurrection of Jesus Christ, who was declared to be the Son of God by the resurrection from the dead (Rom. 1:4).

A Bible dictionary is helpful to understanding key words in the original languages in which the Bible was written, to bring out the richness and accuracy of the biblical accounts. It is far better to use a Hebrew or Greek dictionary to aid you in your Bible studies for it will give you a depth of understanding that would otherwise elude you if you depended solely on an English dictionary. For example, Luke 1:17 describes John's purpose for ministry in the spirit of Elias:

"And he shall go before him in the spirit and power of Elias, to turn the hearts of the fathers to the children, and the disobedient to the wisdom of the just; to make ready a people prepared for the Lord."

The keyword chosen for word study is "wisdom," and the term "wisdom" is from the Greek: "phronesis". It denotes practical wisdom, a wisdom that compels you to act in a certain way that, in context, corresponds to the nature of the righteous. The term comes from its Greek root: "phren", meaning mind, and it refers to the right use of the mind – a mindset that signifies a fixed mental attitude or disposition that determines how one behaves. To change your behaviour for the better is going to require a change of mindset.

Another instance of doing word studies is in Luke 1:37 where the angel Gabriel said to Mary,

"For with God nothing shall be impossible."

In the Greek language of this verse, the angel communicated a profound and striking truth that was diluted by the English translation. The angel literally said, "oti ouk adunatesei to para theo pan rhema", which translates in English: "every word from God shall not be without power." Then Mary's response to the angel's message was:

"...Behold the handmaid of the Lord; be it unto me according to thy word" (v38).

She locked onto the fact that her miraculous conception would not come by the seed of man but by the seed of the Word and the Spirit. So, studies of keywords in the original languages of the Bible are effective tools for biblical interpretation.

Another principle for Bible interpretation is understanding the relationship between the Old and New Testaments. They are not contradictory but complementary Covenants. The Old is the foundation of the New and the New is the completion and fulfilment of the Old. Things in the Old Testament were physical illustrations known as types and shadows which pointed to spiritual realities in the New Testament (Col. 2:16-17; Heb. 10:1). For example, the Apostle John describes the incarnation of Christ saying,

"And the Word was made flesh, and dwelt among us..." (Jn. 1:14a).

The word "dwelt" is from the Greek verb "eskenosen", meaning tabernacled. John was using Old Testament terminology to describe the true reality. In Old Testament times, God commanded Moses to make and erect a tent or tabernacle for His Presence to dwell. By this, God dwelt among His people. God's intention was never to dwell in tents or temples erected by man; it was only an illustration – a type or shadow - of His true desire to be tabernacled in flesh and dwell among us. This was fulfilled and John used the term to convey that fact.

Furthermore terms such as sacrifices, Temple, sin-offerings, priesthood, kingdom, firstfruits, Passover, Pentecost etc. are summarised by New Testament writers to depict some spiritual reality. The New Testament is written in such a way that it assumes its readers already have a good knowledge of the Old Testament. Understanding the Jewish religion, culture, social life, history and languages with its idioms and usages will aid you in interpreting the Word of God accurately. Study aids are intended to help you bridge the gap between the ancient world and the contemporary times in which we live. Here are some study aids to help you get started if you do not already have them: Vine's Expository Dictionary, Unger's Bible Dictionary, Strong's Concordance, Hebrew-Greek Interlinear Bible, Gesenius Hebrew Lexicon, Thayer's Greek Lexicon, Amplified Bible and

Bible commentaries.

10

Meditating the Word

"But his delight is in the law of the LORD, and in his law doth he meditate day and night" (Ps. 1:2).

This verse of scripture reveals the root of a blessed man and a godly life: he delights in the Word of God and in it he meditates day and night; a twofold attitude that is the cause of shaping a person's character with the Word of God at the centre of his life. The practice of paying attention to the Word is a lifestyle; he does not do it now and then, but rather it is a discipline that has inundated his whole life. The verse uses present tense verbs to show that this godly person continuously practices delighting and meditating in the Word of God and then enforces them with the phrase, "day and night". If you delight in the Word, you will meditate in it day and night. In this chapter, I will be looking at the discipline and power of Word-meditation and how it impacts on the whole life of a Christian.

About 3000 years ago, the wise man, King Solomon, penned

these words: "For as he thinketh in his heart, so is he..." (Prov. 23:7). Your heart – the core and centre of your being – determines who you are, and who you are defines your behaviour. Additionally, how you behave determines your destiny, but this chain of cause and effect is linked all the way back to the first cause: how you think. A knock-on effect is therefore created, whereby your thinking, choices, actions, habits, character and destiny are inextricably linked; each feeding off what has been preceded. If you want to change your destiny, change the way that you think and do it with the Word of God. This is the recipe for success in the Kingdom of God.

The Lord gave Joshua the key to a successful, prosperous life from His perspective and it states,

"This book of the law shall not depart from thy mouth; but thou shalt meditate therein day and night, that thou mayest observe to do according to all that is written therein: for then thou shalt make thy way prosperous, and then thou shalt have good success" (Josh. 1:8).

In the previous chapter, I dealt with the importance of studying the Word of God. However, there is another discipline that is complementary to it that will transition you from merely hearing the Word to doing the Word, and that is meditation. You will only be blessed or empowered in doing the Word, not merely hearing it (Ja. 1:25).

Joshua 1:8 shows us that meditation is concomitant with speaking God's Word out of your mouth. In other words, meditation involves speaking. The Hebrew word for "meditate" is "haga", and it means to utter, mutter, whisper; the low sound of the moaning of a dove (Is. 38:14; 59:11) to the loud sound of the growling of a lion over its prey (Is. 31:4). It means to ponder, meditate and devise. The passage of scripture is exhorting us to meditate by speaking for this will enable us to capture the Word of God and release it into our life and change us, our circumstances, and our destiny.

Set aside time to utter, mutter, whisper and shout the Word out of your mouth, for it will establish and reshape your thoughts with God's thoughts and determine your behaviour and character to line up with God's Word. Your mind and mouth are tools and instruments of spiritual transformation. This is what you do to change the way you think, and in so doing, you will be transformed. Joshua 1:8 tells us that meditation with speaking empowers you to obey God's Word:

"This book of the law shall not depart out of thy mouth: but thou shalt meditate therein day and night THAT THOU MAYEST OBSERVE TO DO..."

Meditation is the catalyst for obedience because your behaviour is shaped by your thought-life. If you want to change what you are doing, feed your thought life through meditating on the Word of God. Write the Word upon your mind and heart through meditation and speaking. The psalmist declares,

"My heart is inditing a good matter. I speak of the things which I have made touching the king: my tongue is the pen of a ready writer" (Ps. 45:1).

Every seed in thought and word will produce after its own kind. Your walk will be determined by what you think. The Apostle

Paul says,

"For they that are after the flesh do mind the things of the flesh; but they that are after the Spirit the things of the Spirit. For to be carnally minded is death; but to be spiritually minded is life and peace" (Rom. 8:5-6).

One's walk in the flesh is a result of thinking on fleshly things and conversely, one's walk in the Spirit will be the result of thinking and meditating on the things of the Spirit. The former is being carnally minded, but the latter is being spiritually minded – two opposing principles. Transitioning from one to the other will come about by what you set your mind on. The Apostle Paul exhorts us,

"Be not conformed to this world: but be ye transformed by the renewing of your mind, that ye may prove what is that good, and acceptable, and perfect will of God" (Rom. 12:2).

In order not to be fashioned according to the character, behavioural patterns and customs of the world, you must be transformed – changed from the inside out – how? By the renewing of the mind, which is, replacing old, ungodly thought-patterns with new ones by feeding and exposing your thoughts to God's Word through meditation. What you consider and think on long enough, you'll become. When you accept whatever God's Word says as the final authority in your life and begin to pray over it and meditate on it, muttering, uttering and speaking His Word over yourself and your situation, you will be metamorphosed into the very thing you are considering. Then, you will be able to prove what is that good and acceptable and perfect will of God.

The greatest enemy to a believer is what is lurking in the dark area of the mind that needs to be exposed for what it is, by the light of God's Word (Ps.'s119:105, 30). Once it is exposed, pull down that stronghold that is hindering you from doing God's will, through meditation and prayer. This is the essence of spiritual warfare confirmed by the Word of God:

"For though we walk in the flesh, we do not war after the flesh: (for the weapons of our warfare are not carnal, but mighty through God to the pulling down of strongholds;) Casting down imaginations, and every high thing that exalteth itself against the knowledge of God, and bringing into captivity every thought to the obedience of Christ; And having in a readiness to revenge all disobedience, when your obedience is fulfilled" (2 Cor. 10:3-6).

This passage of scripture shows us that the key to walking in victory and obedience is to pull down and destroy strongholds which are imaginations, reasoning and exalted thought-patterns that are contrary to the knowledge of God's Word.

In today's society, Christians are being bombarded with ungodly images and information from people, television, radio, magazines and newspapers, the music industry and the internet, and in order to protect the heart, you must be careful that the wrong images and information don't get in and entertain your thoughts. The Bible states,

"Finally, brethren, whatsoever things are true, whatsoever things are honest, whatsoever things are just, whatsoever things are pure, whatsoever things are lovely, whatsoever things are of good report; if there be any virtue, and if there be any praise, think on these things. Those things, which ye have learned, and received, and heard, and seen in me, do: and the God of peace shall be with you" (Phil. 4:8-9).

As we meditate upon the right things and cut ourselves off from the wrong images and information, the God of peace, safety, prosperity, wellbeing, health and completeness shall garrison your mind and heart (v7), and revenge all disobedience when you have brought every thought into captivity to the obedience of Christ. What you do will be dependent on the focus of your meditation.

Thoughts are seeds that will produce fruit once they are sown and cultivated through meditation and speaking. Cultivate God's thoughts – His Word - in your heart through meditative utterance so that the Word of God will appear as abundant fruit in your life. This reminds me of the Apostle Paul's encouragement to young Timothy:

"Meditate upon these things; give thyself wholly to them; that thy profiting [progress] may appear to all" (1 Tim. 4:15).

When you continue to meditate in the Word, people will eventually see your spiritual progress shine forth in your life. As you apply yourself to the Word, the Bible says that you will make your way prosperous and you shall have good success. Notice Joshua 1:8 did not say that God would make you prosperous and give you good success - No! God has already made you prosperous and successful. You have to apply yourself to meditate that Word and you will make prosperity and success a reality in your life for all to see.

The blessed man in Psalm 1:1-2 was able to avoid the counsel of the ungodly, the way of sinners and the seat of the scornful because he delighted in the Law of the Lord and meditated in it day and night. Verse 1 negatively characterises the godly man by what he does not do;

"Blessed is the man that walketh not in the counsel of the ungodly, nor standeth in the way of sinners, nor sitteth in the seat of the scornful."

He refuses to do wrong because he has chosen to do right, namely to delight and meditate in the Word of God day and night; and so is characterised positively by what he does. Then verse 3 describes what he is like:

"And he shall be like a tree planted by the rivers of water, that bringeth forth his fruit in his season; his leaf also shall not wither; and whatsoever he doeth shall prosper."

These are the evidence of a blessed man who delights and meditates in the Word. He shall be strong and securely rooted like a tree, will not be driven along by every wind of doctrine or weakened by adversity, but will stand strong and unmoved because the Word of God is deeply rooted in him. He will constantly be refreshed by the fountain of living waters because he is in close spiritual proximity to his Source. His leaf also not withering, signifies continual health, vitality and longevity. He will be fruitful, productive and mature in season and will not produce ahead of God's season and timing. Everything he puts his hand to will prosper as also stated in Joshua 1:8.

For anything that you need to change in your life, go to the Word and find verses of scripture that cover your situation.

Itemise those verses in a list on a piece of paper or card. Then every day read and speak them to yourself, pondering them in your mind. Doing so will allow the Word of God to grow in your spirit until it saturates your whole being.

11

Spiritual Warfare

"For we wrestle not against flesh and blood, but against principalities, against powers, against the rulers of the darkness of this world, against spiritual wickedness in high places" (Eph. 6:13).

We live in a hostile world fraught with antagonistic influences such as wars, hatred, sexual immorality, theft, murders, violence, sickness and diseases, natural disasters and much more. These are on the increase as we approach the imminent coming of Christ. These calamitous events are driven by wicked invisible forces that use human instrumentality to achieve their evil plots.

Through the redemptive blood of Christ we were translated from the authority of darkness into the Kingdom of God's dear Son (Col. 1:13). God has assigned us as soldiers to engage in battle against the forces of evil to defend your position and to go on the offensive to deliver others from the oppression of the Devil (Ac. 10:38). The intent of spiritual warfare in the life of believers is not to obtain the victory but rather to enforce the victory that they already have in Christ Jesus, who obtained it for us by the blood of His cross (Col. 2:14-15; Heb. 2:14-15).

We have already become partakers of Christ's victory by identification with Him in His death, burial, resurrection and ascension, which occurred when we were born again (Rom. 6:3-6; Eph. 2:5-6). Therefore, we are to engage, not in a fight to obtain the victory, but in the good fight of faith that testifies to the reality that we already have the victory and we must keep laying hold of it. 1 John 5:4-5 declares,

"For whatsoever is born of God overcometh the world: and this is the victory that overcometh the world, even our faith. Who is he that overcometh the world, but he that believeth that Jesus is the Son of God?"

If you believe with your heart that Jesus is the Son of God, you already have the victory - the faith that overcomes the world. And so, the Bible instructs us to fight the good fight of faith and to lay hold on eternal life (1 Tim. 6:12). Satan's strategy is to entice you to give up what Jesus purchased for you so that he can have access to your life, to steal, kill and destroy (Jn. 10:10).

In the spiritual warfare passage of Ephesians 6:10-18, the Apostle Paul lays down the truths and strategies for engagement with the archenemy. He begins by introducing a divine injunction that is imperative for success in battle:

"Finally, my brethren, be strong in the Lord, and in the power of his might" (Eph. 6:10).

Spiritual Warfare

Being strong in our own might is definitely no match for the Devil and is a prediction of guaranteed failure. However, to succeed in battle, you must follow the injunction to be strong in the Lord: that is in your relationship with the Lord who is all-powerful and has defeated the Devil and his cohorts. It also signifies your union and identification in His victory over the authority of darkness. Now how do you become strong in the Lord and in the power of His might?

There are three aspects of divine enablement identified by the synonyms: strong, power and might. The term "strong" is translated from the Greek word "dunamis", which means inherent power, force or strength, a by-product of the baptism in the Holy Spirit according to Acts 1:8,

"But ye shall receive power, after that the Holy Ghost is come upon you: and ye shall be witnesses unto me both in Jerusalem, and in all Judea, and in Samaria, and unto the utmost part of the earth."

On receiving the Holy Spirit, you have inherent power abiding on the inside of you. We are empowered as witnesses of Jesus Christ, equipped to overcome the powers of darkness in times of trials and temptations. We are also endowed with the ability to cast out demons, heal the sick and raise the dead (Matt. 10:7-8; Mk. 16:15-20; Lk. 10:17-19); to enforce Satan's defeat and Christ's victory.

The second synonym is "power" and is translated from the Greek word "kratos", denoting force, strength, might. It especially signifies manifested power, and is derived from the root "kra", to perfect or complete. It is possible to have inherent power resident on the inside of a Spirit-filled person, and yet, that power is doing little more than nothing because it is lying dormant and needs to be stirred up (2 Tim. 1:6). To be baptised in the Holy Spirit is wonderful, but that power in you must be stirred up and used or else you will be ineffective. So Ephesians 6: 10 is not only instructing us to have inherent power but also to manifest that power in our every day lives and perfect or complete the purpose for which it was given; hence, the Greek term used to depict manifested power.

The term "might" is also used, translated from the Greek word "ischus", and signifies power as an endowment. "Endow", according to the Collins Dictionary, means "to provide with or bequeath a permanent source of income". In this instance, I am talking about being provided with a permanent source of divine power: the Holy Spirit. There is no need to look to our own strength, but to the strength of the Divine One who lives on the inside of us (1 Jn. 4:4). We have a divine enablement that has been bequeathed to us as heirs of God and joint-heirs with Christ (Rom. 8:17).

You have all that you need to overcome sin, the flesh and the Devil, for the Lord has become your Strength (Ps. 27:1) The same injunction given in Ephesians 6:10 was also given in Joshua 1 at the outset of Israel's military conquest. The underlying key to strength and courage is to meditate in the Word day and night (v8), as was covered in the preceding chapter of this book.

Verse 11-12 of Ephesians 6 informs us as to what and who we battle against:

"Put on the whole armour of God, that ye may be able stand

against the wiles of the devil. For we wrestle not against flesh and blood, but against principalities, against powers, against the rulers of the darkness of this world, against spiritual wickedness in high places."

The first question is what are we fighting against? We are engaged in warfare against the wiles of the Devil. The term "wiles" is from the Greek word "methodia", and denotes craftiness, deceit, lies, cunning devices, trickery. This word is used in Ephesians 4:14 and literally means "with a view to the craft of deceit" (Vine 1985 p 216). Every believer is in a fight against Satan's lies, deceit and crafty devices. We are not fighting Satan and his cohorts per se, for he is a defeated foe, but we are fighting against his lies and deceit. So when the Bible refers to us wrestling against Satan's host of wicked spirits, that is merely in relation to their lies, cunning devices and trickery. These lies, deceit and cunning craftiness suggest that their primary purpose is to attack and infiltrate the mind, which is the doorway to the heart. Therefore, these wiles and crafty deceit are essentially ungodly and wicked thought patterns rooted in temptation to seduce us into believing Satan's lies and trickery.

Therefore, the Apostle admonishes us to put on the whole armour of God that we may be able to stand against the wiles of the Devil. The reason why we can see the devil's destructive ability in the different areas of life in this world is because people have been persuaded with his lies and deceit. That gives him authority in their lives to steal, kill and destroy (Jn. 10:10).

Secondly, who are we fighting against? Paul tells us that we are wrestling against principalities, against powers, against the rulers of the darkness of this world and against spiritual wickedness in high places. The Apostle Paul presents the hierarchical structure of Satan's kingdom that is in opposition to the Kingdom of God. Retrospectively, the Christian soldier wrestles against them, in so far as it relates to their lies, craftiness, tricks and deceit. Furthermore, it is important to correctly understand that you cannot stop the attacks and bombardment of evil, deceitful and enticing thoughts, but you can stop them from infiltrating your heart.

There are four hierarchical levels of Satan's kingdom outlined by the Apostle Paul in verse 12. He first identifies our true enemies as not being flesh and blood like you and me, but unseen spiritual beings. These are classified into four groups beginning from the lowest to the highest rank of angelic beings: wicked spirits in the heavenlies.

The term "principalities", is from the Greek rendering "archas", signifying beginning, government, rule; this refers to supramundane beings who exercise rule. The next level of rank are "powers", from which we get the Greek term "exousias", meaning authorities. These fallen angelic beings delegate authority to principalities to enforce their will. And then the higher rank of fallen angels are called the rulers of the darkness of this world. The Greek rendering is "kosmokratoras tou skotous tou aionos", literally translated, "world rulers of the darkness of this age." And the highest rank of fallen angels are designated as spiritual wickedness in high places translated from the Greek: "pneumatika tes ponerias en tois epouraniois, "spirits of wickedness in the heavenlies. These are the wicked spirits who function in the heavenlies. The term "heavenlies" in the Greek (epouraniois), refers to that which pertains to being in the heavens, in contrast to being on the earth.

The Lord revealed to Kenneth Hagin how the kingdom of darkness functions and its hierarchical structure: the lowest leadership rank, mentioned in Ehesians 6:12, being principalities, and the highest being wicked spirits in heavenly places. Jesus showed him how to deal with the first three ranks as they pertain to the earth, and he asked the Lord,

"Lord, You have told me about only three categories of evil spirits: the rulers of the darkness of this world, the powers, and the principalities. What about the wicked spirits in the heavenlies"? Jesus replied, "You take care of the ones on earth. I will take care of those in the heavenlies" (Hagin 2002 p81).

Jesus Christ delegated His authority on the earth to His Church and retained His authority in heaven so that what we bind on earth will be also bound in heaven (Matt. 16:19; 18:18; 28:18-20). Therefore, we are authorised to resist and remove sin on the earth through the preaching and teaching of the Word; to cast out devils and heal all manner of sicknesses and diseases (Matt. 10:1, 7-8; 29:18-20; Mk. 16:15-20).

Humanity is not the enemy we are fighting against. Most of humanity is held captive by Satan who seeks to ultimately destroy. Moreover, human beings are generally used as pawns by Satan to perpetuate his wicked and evil devices, because they are blinded by him (2 Cor. 4:4; Rev. 12:9). Satan and his cohorts of demons and fallen angels cannot force their way into our lives to influence and control us, and eventually destroy us. His only strategy used to try and gain access to control and destroy us, is deception. If we yield to his deception by believing his lies, he then sets up strongholds in our minds by which to influence, control and destroy us. The battlefield of spiritual warfare is in the mind. That is the place where you win or lose; it is the number one target the enemy aims at because once he has your mind, he has you, and therefore can control your life. Your mind is the doorway into your heart. If he has your mind, he has your heart also.

Satan and his devils have control of peoples' lives through strongholds: the ungodly thought-processes of the mind. To break free from Satan's control and bondage, you must pull down and destroy those very strongholds: those unholy thought-patterns. The Apostle tells us that,

"(For the weapons of our warfare are not carnal, but mighty through God to the pulling down of strong holds;) Casting down imaginations, and every high thing that exalteth itself against the knowledge of God, and bringing into captivity every thought to the obedience of Christ (2 Cor. 10:4-5).

In this verse lies the progression of thoughts becoming strongholds in the mind, whereby thoughts become imaginations or reasonings; a reasoning becomes a high or exalted thing, and an exalted thing becomes a stronghold.

Every temptation begins with a thought. You cannot stop a thought from coming to your mind, but you can stop an evil thought from staying in your mind by refusing to entertain it. It is said that you cannot stop a bird from flying over your head, but you can stop a bird from making a nest in your hair. To have an evil thought in your mind is not sin, it becomes sin when you engage with it through meditation.

The second stage is imaginations translated from the Greek word "logismos", and it suggests a mental contemplation of evil intent that comes by reasonings, arguments and pondering. When one considers, ponders, entertains and meditates on an evil thought or idea, it will eventually get into the core of your being – the heart – and defile it. What you think on continuously will become so magnified and enlarged in your own mind, that it becomes sin.

Ungodly thoughts are magnified and exalted in one's own mind when you think, reason and ponder on it. Then it becomes an high or exalted thing that is elevated against the knowledge of God's Word. At this point, the Word of God has ceased to be the final authority in your life. An ungodly thought-pattern becomes more important than the Word of God. Why? Because it is now an exalted thing.

When thoughts are exalted, they are built up to become strongholds in the mind that the Enemy can oppress, torment and exercise control over you. Demons operate and hide behind the strongholds of erroneous, sinful, habitual thought patterns. To first deal with these strongholds, you must identify and expose them to the Light of God's Word (Ps. 119:105, 130).

God's Word is Light

These strongholds exist in the darkness, and therefore, need to be exposed by the Light of the Word. The Bible says that the entrance of God's Word gives light, it gives understanding unto the simple (Ps. 119:130). Your darkness is your area of ignorance. Light signifies revelation knowledge, understanding and illumination. When you walk in the light of understanding, you cannot be overcome by the wicked one. As he and his cohorts can only rule in an atmosphere of darkness, that is why they are the rulers of the darkness of this world (Eph. 6:12). In the Light, they have no power over you. Hence, it is important that you saturate yourself with the truth: the Word of God.

The first piece of Christian armour mentioned to counteract the lies, deception and trickery of the Devil is to have your loins girded about with the girdle (or belt) of truth. The Apostle Peter shows us where to put the girdle of truth:

"Wherefore, gird up the loins of your mind..." (1 Pe. 1:13a).

The "loins" in biblical terminology denoted, in a natural sense, the reproductive organs and their creative power for life (Ac.2:30; Heb. 7:5). In a spiritual sense, when this scripture refers to the loins of the mind, the Holy Spirit is conveying that your mind possesses the creative power for life, success and spiritual fulfilment in the Kingdom of God; so gird your loins with the girdle of truth. What you focus on in your mind will be created for you by God for good. Conversely, if you focus on the evil or the things that contradict divine truth, such things will come into being by the powers of darkness. Girding the loins indicates readiness for active service or to perform some specific task (Ex. 12:11; Lk. 12:35-36). The Apostle Peter shows us how we need to be prepared, ready and sober while awaiting the appearing of our Lord Jesus Christ.

We are instructed by the Apostle Paul to put on the breastplate of righteousness. A breastplate protected the vital organs of the body. As these organs were central to the function of the whole body, similarly, righteousness is also central to the life of a believer. Having a righteousness conscious attitude will protect the heart from living in the condemnation of the Devil just as a literal breastplate protects the heart from incoming missiles. For the breastplate of righteousness to work on your behalf, you must recognise that righteousness is a gift (Rom. 5:17); you cannot do anything to earn it. It is received by faith. Additionally, the righteousness you received by faith is the righteousness of God in Christ (2 Cor. 5:21). You did not do anything to obtain it, neither can you do anything to keep it. It was received by faith, therefore it can only be kept by faith in the finished work of the Cross (Rom. 5:9; 1 Pe. 1:5). We overcome Satan's accusations by focusing on the blood of the Lamb and testifying to what it has bought for us (1 Jn. 1:7, 9; Rev. 12:10-11).

Your feet must be shod (or bound) with the preparation of the gospel of peace (v15). Be always ready to use your feet to carry the message of the gospel of peace to a lost world through evangelism (see Rom. 10:15; 1 Pe. 3:15). Preaching or sharing the gospel is part of spiritual warfare. It is going on an offensive attack to demolish and destroy strongholds in people's minds by exposing the light of the Word on them and setting people free from Satanic captivity (2 Cor.4:3-4). With the preaching of the gospel, we are to cast out demons and heal every sickness (Matt. 10:1, 7-8; Mk. 16:15-20). This is how you invade Satanic territories.

Verse 16 admonishes us above everything else, to take up the shield of faith, so that we may be able to quench the fiery darts of the wicked. Faith must be taken into consideration above everything else because you cannot possess the truth without faith; you cannot have righteousness without it; neither can you have a firm footing with the gospel of peace without faith; nor can you wield the sword of the Spirit apart from faith; and lastly, you cannot be saved without faith. Everything that is obtained or functions in the Kingdom of God is by faith. So the shield of faith stands above everything else. The imagery here is of a wet shield that has been soaked in water for the purpose of quenching the fiery missiles of the enemy – a common practice among the Romans with wooden shields. The spiritual shield of faith is to be doused in the water of the Word (Eph. 5:27) for faith comes by hearing and hearing by the Word of God. Keep our faith soaked in the Word of God so that you are able to quench the fiery wiles and trickery of the Devil. Without faith, you cannot even begin to engage in spiritual warfare because the nature of this warfare is a fight of faith (1 Tim. 6:12).

The helmet of salvation (v17) is referred to by the Apostle Paul as the hope of salvation in (1 Thess. 5:8). Hope is the earnest expectation of something good. This helmet of the hope of salvation is the earnest and joyful expectation of our ultimate deliverance at the appearing of Jesus Christ. This hope is purifies and sustains us in our trials and tribulations that face us in life (Rom. 8:24-25; 1 Jn. 3:2-3). Hope gives us an inward vision of what we do not see, as yet, with the optical eyes but waits joyfully for its manifestation to the natural senses. Keep your hope alive through the Word (Rom. 15:4) and hold fast to the promises God made to you that has not yet come to visible manifestation, and don't allow the enemy to rob you of your hope.

Lastly, we are instructed to take the sword of the Spirit, which is the Word of God. The Greek term for "word" is "rhema", and it means that which is spoken or uttered. To wield the sword of the Spirit, you must open your mouth and speak to that adverse situation that is confronting you whether temptation to sin, demons, sickness and disease etc. Secondly, the rhema of God refers to a specific individual word or scripture that the Spirit has quickened to you. Jesus used three specific scriptures (Matt. 4) to counteract the temptations of the Devil by speaking them out prefaced with "it is written. That is what you need to do when you are tempted. Resist the Devil with the rhema of God, the sword of the Spirit, and he will flee from you (Ja. 4:7). The words Jesus spoke were spirit and life (Jn. 6:63). Studying God's Word equips you with the ability to use the Word skilfully. Learn the promises that cover every possible situation you'll come up against in the future or it may be a situation you are going through presently.

Finally, the rhema of God can be a command or word of faith spoken into a situation that you want to change. Jesus taught His disciples to speak to the mountain without doubting in their hearts as He did the fig tree (Matt. 21:20-21; Mk. 12:21-23). The word "mouth" is the same in Greek as that which is translated to mean, the edge of a weapon. Your mouth is the weapon that releases the sword of the Spirit: the rhema of God and no rhema from God shall be without power (Lk. 1:37 Gk).

12

The Assembly of the Saints

"Not forsaking the assembling of ourselves together, as the manner of some is; but exhorting one another: and so much the more, as ye see the day approaching" (Heb. 10:25).

The opening scripture presented by the Hebrew writer is not an option but a divine injunction for every born again believer to obey. There are some Christians today who think that they do not need to go to church. They will say that you do not need to go to church to serve God, or you do not need to go to church to become a Christian. That is true at the initial stage of walking with the Lord. However, you will need to go to church to become and a strong, vibrant Christian for the Kingdom of God. I want to explore in this chapter, the spiritual benefits and importance of being committed to a church fellowship and how it can enhance spiritual growth.

To apprehend and appreciate the importance of church-life, we must first understand the true nature of the Church from the

Word of God. The Church was not a human idea, it was God's idea, ordained before the foundation of the world. The Apostle Paul defines it as a mystery that was hidden from the beginning of the world but is now revealed by the Spirit saying,

"How that by revelation he made known unto me the mystery; (as I wrote afore in few words, Whereby, when ye read, ye may understand my knowledge in the mystery of Christ) Which in other ages was not made known unto the sons of men, as it is now revealed unto his holy apostles and prophets by Spirit; That the Gentiles should be fellowheirs, and of the same body, and partakers of his promise in Christ by the gospel ... And to make all men see what is the fellowship of the mystery, which from the beginning of the world hath been hid in God, who created all things by Jesus Christ" (Eph. 3:3-6, 9).

God's plan from the beginning, is that there should be a Church in this world. When I say "Church", I am not talking about a literal physical building, but an assembly of flesh and blood believers called out from the ungodly world to be God's peculiar treasure, hence the Greek term for "church is "ekklesia", meaning an assembly of called out ones. Therefore the biblical meaning of Church refers to God's holy people who join together in fellowship. My definition of Church from the Scriptures is a visible, local assembly of redeemed spirit-filled believers called out to worship God in spirit and in truth.

When New Testament writers were addressing the Church, they wrote letters to local visible assemblies in geographical areas. For example, the Apostle Paul wrote letters to the church at Corinth (1 Cor. 1:1-2; 2 Cor. 1:1) and to local churches or assemblies in Galatia (Gal. 1:1). If the Church was universal and mystical, Paul could not have addressed the people of God at Galatia in the plural sense as distinct local churches. He also addressed the church of the Thessalonians (1 Thess. 1:1; 2 Thess. 1:1) and to Philemon and the church in his house (Philm. 1:1-2). The Apostle John writes to the seven churches of Asia Minor (Rev. 2-3). There is no universal, invisible mystical church that one can belong to without the attendance of a local gathering of believers. People who support this view are those who do not go to a local assembly or are not committed to a local church but tend to visit a variety of local assemblies from time to time.

The command from the Word of God is given "Not to forsake the assembling of ourselves together, as the manner of some is..." Since Jesus Christ promised to build His church (Matt. 16:18). His intention was not for any believer to be isolated from the assembly of the saints. He gives a reason why believers should be gathered together in the preceding verse (v24),

"And let us consider one another to provoke unto love and to good works:

And then the verse after declares that we are not to forsake the assembly of ourselves, but by exhortation, we provoke one another to love and good works as mentioned in verse 24 and 25 of Hebrews 10. God created us to be social beings, not to be an island by ourselves; therefore it is mentally and emotionally unwholesome to live an isolated life. So generally, people will socialise with their peers, whether good or bad, and that company to which they belong, will contribute to the formation of their character. If the company you keep is not conducive to you fulfilling your righteous destiny, it will hinder you. The Bible informs us that evil communication corrupts good manners (1

Cor. 15:33). On the other hand, if you keep company with the spiritually mature, you will take on their mindset and behaviour that will propel you to fulfil your destiny. Nobody in life ever achieves success by themselves; there is always someone with whom you have a close association. In the Book of Proverbs it declares,

"He that walketh with wise men shall be wise: but a companion of fools shall be destroyed" (13:20).

The whole Book of Proverbs describes two contrasting characters: the righteous and the wicked. The righteous is identified as wise, but the wicked as fools (Prov. 1:2-7; 5:1-8). Being committed to a local church for a sufficiently long time, where the Word of God is taught, will help you grow strong spiritually and faster than if you had stayed on your own, merely visiting churches. There surely is a difference between visiting a church and being committed to one. The one who is committed to a church that teaches the Word will be walking with the wise. Notice the present tense verb: "walketh;" he is the one who frequently fellowships with the saints. It is in consistency that the power and stability to become what God has called you to be lie, for change comes with repetition.

On the other hand, the person who visits a church but does not stay around to form a strong vibrant relationship with the saints will end up not having a strong character in his spiritual life. He will miss out on what the Word teaches about the righteous:

"The righteous shall flourish like the palm tree: he shall grow like a cedar in Lebanon. Those that be planted in the house of the LORD shall flourish in the courts of our God. They shall still bring forth fruit in old age; they shall be fat with flourishing" (Ps. 92:12-14).

To flourish, according to the Collins Dictionary, means to prosper, to be healthy, to be in peak condition. And verses 12-13 declare that the righteous who are planted in the house of the Lord shall flourish like the palm trees and grow like a cedar in Lebanon. There are three important things are mentioned in these verses: flourish, growth and fruit in old age. Spiritual growth will be the feature of one who is committed to being a part of the assembly of the saints. God has set pastoral and teaching gifts in the church (Eph. 4:11) for the spiritual growth of the Body. When one commits to a local assembly, thus coming under the oversight and teaching of pastors and elders, there will be spiritual growth and the Christian journey will be made easier because of the support network.

The next feature is that the righteous shall bring forth fruit in old age. This refers to fruitfulness and longevity. A believer who is part of a local assembly that teaches the unadulterated Word, will have the fruit of it produced in his life. This is because he will be inundated with the Word ministry of the leaders, and the ministry of the saints will bring the increase and growth of the Body as the scripture affirms:

"But speaking the truth in love, may grow up into him in all things, which is the head, even Christ: From whom the whole body fitly joined together and compacted by that which every part supplieth, according to the effectual working in the measure of every part, maketh increase of the body unto the edifying of itself in love" (Eph. 4:15-16).

The growth process incorporates our private, personal devotion with God and our communal relationship with the saints. There are things that God will not show you in your personal worship time that he will reveal to you in your pubic fellowship with the saints because he does not want you to become proud or isolated from the assembly of the saints. Generally, there is a greater body of truth amongst the plurality of saints than there is by yourself; and so having interaction with the saints will give you an opportunity to learn and develop. The Apostle Paul declares,

"That Christ may dwell in your hearts by faith; that ye, being rooted and grounded in love, may be able to COMPREHEND WITH ALL SAINTS what is the breadth, and length, and depth, and height" (Eph. 3:17-18).

God wants us as individuals to comprehend with all saints the dimensions of His love so that we may be filled with all the fullness of God (v19). Among the saints there are facets of revelation that you don't know and will not know until you meet those saints. The purpose of fellowship with the saints is so that you may be trained. The bible encourages parents to train up a child in the way that he should go so that when he is old, he will not depart from it. While this is true in the natural, it is also true in the spiritual. The local church is for training. When a saint is trained in the Word of God, he will not depart from it but will continue to bear fruit in old age.

Another benefit of participating in the assembly of the saints is that you will come to discover and function in your gifting. The church of Jesus Christ is called the Body of Christ. Paul uses this term in his epistle to the Corinthians as a metaphor to depict the plurality and diversity of operation of the gifts in the saints. Moreover, the analogy of a body conveys the notion that the gifts are to function within the context of being a part of the Body of Christ, in the same sense that the physical members do function, but not independently of the body. The Apostle, after listing the nine gifts of the Spirit states,

"For as the body is one, and hath many members, and all the members of that one body, being many, are one body: so also is Christ" (1 Cor. 12:12).

As a simple explanation of what this verse is saying, what is true about the nature of your physical body – its plurality of members, diversity of functions and corporate unity – is also a reflection of Christ: that is His Body: the Church. Then Paul confirms that he is addressing the Corinthian saints to be the Body of Christ in the next verse:

"For by one Spirit are we all baptized into one body, whether we be Jews or Gentiles, whether we be bond or free; and have been all made to drink into one Spirit" (v13).

It is by the one Spirit that we have been baptised into one body irrespective of our ethnicity, nationality or social status. We are made alive in Christ by the Spirit (Jn. 3:3-5; 2 Cor. 5:17; Titus 3:5) and placed in the Body of Christ to give and to receive spiritual nourishment from Christ through the Body (Col. 2:19). God's plan was to position you in the Body as it pleases Him. Setting you in the Body will also include the depositing of a gift or gifts within you, so that as you exercise them, these gifts will contribute to the building up of the saints of Jesus Christ. In verse 18 it declares,

"But now hath God set the members every one of them in the

body, as it hath pleased Him."

Notice the verse states that God has set every one of them in the body without exception. So if you are born again and you are not attending a local assembly, you need to find out what local church has God planned for you to be a part of and what gift has he positioned you to function in. For verse 28 declares,

"And God has set some in the church, first apostles, secondarily prophets, thirdly teachers, after that miracles, then gifts of healings, helps, governments, diversities of tongues."

We all do not have the same gifts for we are a body. The whole body is not an eye or an ear but one Body with many members and all those members have different functions. Therefore, being committed to a local assembly will give God the opportunity to teach you what your gifting is and to begin to function in that calling so that the Body may receive edification. Discovering who you are and what you were born to accomplish will come to fruition when you see the major importance of going to church. If Jesus Himself, the Son of the living God, attended a local Jewish synagogue as was His custom (Lk. 4:16), how much more you. Jesus' attendance at the local Jewish gathering as well as at the Temple in Jerusalem was part of His preparation for future ministry. In actual fact, when he was twelve years of age, he went with His parents to Jerusalem to observe the Jewish feast of Passover; He tarried there after His parents had long gone; they supposing he had been with them, but consequently returned to look for Him. When they had found Him, they informed Him that they searched for Him, but Jesus' reply recorded in Luke 2:49 was this:

"...How is it that ye sought me? Wist ye not that I must be about my father's business?"

Jesus deemed His attendance at the Temple in Jerusalem as well as His discussions among the doctors of the Law as being about His Father's business. His attendance at the national gathering of the Jews was in obedience to the Scriptures (Ex. 23:14-17). Similarly, let us not forsake the assembly of the saints in obedience to the Word of God. Exhort and receive exhortation from the saints even much more for the Day of the Lord is approaching. Now hear the resounding words of the Prophet Malachi of those who exhort one another to provoke unto love and good works:

"Then they that feared the LORD spake often one to another: and the LORD hearkened, and heard it, and a book of remembrance was written before him for them that feared the LORD, and that thought upon his name. And they shall be mine, saith the LORD of host, in that day when I make up my jewels; and I will spare them, as a man spareth his own son that serveth him. Then shall ye return, and discern between the righteous and the wicked, between him that serveth God and him that serveth him not" (Mal.3:16-18).

Bibliography

Edersheim, A (1994) "The Temple: Its Ministry and Services" Hendrickson Publishers Inc Peabody, Massachusetts, USA

Hagin, K E (2002) "I believe in Visions" Faith Library Publications: Tulsa, Oklahoma

Vine, W. E. (1985) "An Expository Dictionary of New Testament Words," Moody Press: Chicago

www.ingramcontent.com/pod-product-compliance
Lightning Source LLC
Chambersburg PA
CBHW021131300426
44113CB00006B/382